new Tapas

TODAY'S BEST BAR FOOD FROM SPAIN

SANTA MARIA # 65

- Chips de yuca 375
- Anchoas con pan con tomate 675
- Hojama de atún con cebolla tierna y aceite de oliva 675
- Cecina de león 775
- Ensalada de castañas y calabaza y queso feta 675
- "Ravillons" con apio y mantequilla de cacahuete en ensalada 775
- Empanadillas de setas y pato confitado 415
- Ancas de rana marinadas con salvia y gengibre 675
- Guiso de caracoles con tortilla japonesa 690
- Sushi de verdunas con salvia 925
- Maki de aguacate y pepino 750
- Maki de gamba y lechón rebozado 1100
- Sushi variado 2500
- Huevas de codorniz escalfados con pisto y chistorra 450
- "Ravillons botó" a la plancha 900
- Alcachofas guisadas con berengenas 625
- Tian tan de verdura 675
- Salteado de arroz integral con shitake, espárragos y judías 625
- Truchas de río con acelga, champiñones y cecina 675
- Bacalao con bonito y encurtidos 775
- Pichón con manzana 875
- Costillas de ternera, col lombarda y patata 850
- Hígado de pato con pera y pimienta sichuan 800
- Alitas de pollo tandoni 475
- Surtido de quesos 675

※ A partir de 5 comensales sólo se sirve menu degustación ※

═ Postres ═

- Piña colada con chupa-chups 450
- Helado de caki, plumb-cake y toffe 675
- Manzana reineta con bizcocho de frutos secos y helado de chocolate 675
- Trufas de chocolate 375

FIONA DUNLOP

new Tapas

TODAY'S BEST BAR FOOD FROM SPAIN

MITCHELL BEAZLEY

To the fast-developing taste-buds of Oskar and Archie

THE BASQUE REGION 9

CATALONIA 33

RIOJA and OLD CASTILE 65

NEW TAPAS by Fiona Dunlop
First published in Great Britain in 2002 by Mitchell Beazley, an imprint of Octopus Publishing Group Limited, 2-4 Heron Quays, London E14 4JP.
Reprinted 2003
© Octopus Publishing Group Limited 2002
Text (except recipes) © Fiona Dunlop 2002 All rights reserved. No part of this publication may be reproduced or utilised in any form by any means, electronic or mechanical, including photocopying, recording, or by any information storage and retrieval system, without prior written permission of the publishers. A CIP catalogue record for this book is available from the British Library. The author and publisher will be grateful for any information that will assist in keeping future editions up to date.

ISBN 1 84000 578 5

While all reasonable care has been taken during the preparation of this edition, neither the publisher nor the author can accept responsibility for any consequences arising from the use thereof or from the information contained therein.

Commissioning Editor: Rebecca Spry Art Editor: Nicky Collings Design: Vanessa Courtier Photography: Jan Baldwin Editors: Jamie Ambrose, Hattie Ellis and Rebecca Spry Recipe tester: Diana Henry Recipe translator: Ana Sims Production: Alix McCulloch Index: John Noble
Typeset in Interstate Printed and bound by Toppan Printing Company in China

CONTENTS

INTRODUCTION

In the last decade or so, tapas have conquered the world, radiating from their Hispanic source to tease the taste-buds of anyone in search of a generous snack to accompany a glass of wine. Yet such pan-national culinary clones are mere shadows of the real thing, which is only found in Spain itself. Racy flavours, high contrasts, generous doses of virgin olive oil, ultra-fresh ingredients, fearless use of offal and obsessive use of salt cod or cured ham – these are just some of the hallmarks of Spanish tapas. Somehow, this gastronomic dance is not far from the emotional highs and lows and the syncopated rhythms of flamenco – the iconic representation of Spain itself.

Naturally enough, much tipsy speculation has taken place over the origins of tapas. Linguistically, the meaning is an extension of the word *tapa* ('lid'), from *tapar* ('to cover'), allegedly referring to slices of cheese or ham used to cover glasses of sherry in the hot, insect-infested bars of Andalucía. From these prosaic beginnings, so the story goes, came the tradition of serving small portions of bar food free with a glass of beer, wine or sherry. An alternative theory stems from the 13th century, when the Castilian King Alfonso X, surrendering to doctor's orders to recuperate from an illness, spent long days in bed, sipping small glasses of restorative wine accompanied by reduced portions of food. His recovery was so painless that there soon followed a royal decree ordering taverns to only serve wine if accompanied by a snack. Yet another, more down-to-earth, theory equates tapas with the punctuations of the rural working day, tiding over

appetites and boosting energy in a climate not always conducive to huge meals or hard labour. Pre- or post-*siesta*, grazing was the way to go for Spain's agricultural masses.

Whatever their starting point, tapas have moved on and are now inextricably linked to the Spanish way of life. They have generated the *tapeo* (tapas bar crawl), a unique, mobile institution that brings swarms of families out on to the streets, when the heat of the day has passed, to stroll, chat and stop for a drink and – naturally – a tapa or two. The continuity of the habit is ensured by the presence of many generations, from grandpas to babies, while floors scattered with used napkins, cigarette butts, olive stones, mussel shells and the odd errant anchovy all point clearly to the lip-smacking gusto of the activity.

There is no sitting at isolated tables at the appointed hour, victim to the whims of restaurant staff. The *tapeo* is something else: seemingly spontaneous, convivial and informal, it occurs within customary twice-a-day time-slots on a year-round basis. Ever different, the Basques opt for the word *poteo*, a derivative of *potes* ('pots' or 'jars'), from which wine or cider was once drunk.

Traditionally, each bar cooked up only one speciality, and this enforced peripatetic snacking on a population only too happy to prolong its voluble socialising. Drunkenness is rare; while spirits and decibels soar, excess alcohol is rapidly absorbed by sporadic feeding. You still find one-off house specialities in smaller towns, but today's bars are more likely to chalk up a list of tapas and *raciones* (larger portions) of the day and line up bar-stools so aficionados can eat in comfort using a knife and fork – those little 'lids', after all, are getting bigger and bigger. Again, the exception comes from the Basque Country, where tapas are replaced by *pintxos* (or *pinchos*), finger snacks that resemble French canapés and that are scaling new heights of diversity and elaborateness.

All this is part of the post-Franco ground swell, an awakening to the sophisticated *nueva cocina* (new cuisine)

produce is paramount. The 'rural-folkloric revival' (a term coined by anthropologist T. Seppilli in 1992) is galloping ahead, highlighting local delicacies (anything from a black pudding, a pulse or an organic cured ham to a snail or a quail) that may even be produced in a specific valley or village. This is nurturing a taste for quality. One exception is the ubiquitous *ensaladilla* ('little salad' or Russian salad), a tapa of canned vegetables

'Floors scattered with used paper napkins, cigarette butts, olive stones, mussel shells and the odd errant anchovy all point clearly to the lip-smacking gusto of the activity. There is no sitting around at isolated tables at the appointed hour, victim to the whims of restaurant staff.'

that is galvanising chefs into producing ever-more inventive juxtapositions of ingredients and flavours. The initial impetus came from France via the Basques, and has since conquered local cuisine, from Seville to Barcelona, Madrid to Salamanca. This renaissance has inspired most of this book's recipes, which were created by chefs in search of exciting gastronomic departures. Glutinous bean stews and sad-looking *picadillo* (diced vegetable) salads, move on! There remain, too, the tapas classics, whose earthy flavours are unbeatable reflections of Spanish history, landscapes and produce, and which differ radically from region to region.
Few tapas are universal in Spain; local

smothered in mayonnaise, that just won't go away. For foreigners bemused by its similarity to 1960s airline food, the *ensaladilla* does raise questions as to the gastronomic discernment of this tapa-consuming nation. But then the French still snack on bland *croque monsieur*, so why not? There has to be some sort of atavistic yearning at work here. Mayonnaise itself appears again and again, whether straight out of a jar or as garlic-enhanced *alioli*.

The gastronomic euphoria of the last two decades goes hand-in-hand with Spain's new-found prosperity and awareness of the outside world. These, in turn, have led Spaniards to a greater awareness of their own roots and cultural identity. Regionalism is king and *Denominación de Origen Controllado,* or *DOC*, labels of regulated quality are proliferating; once used only for the country's wines, as *Denominación de Origen (DO)* or with the attached *Calificada (DOCa)* for Rioja, this type of quality control now extends to foodstuffs such as white beans or suckling pigs. Well-travelled chefs now concoct fusion food that in some cases harks back to Spain's complex and cosmopolitan history. The wheel turns full circle to reintegrate Arab contrasts of flavours that were originally brought to the country by the Moors. In the same way, there is a revival of the Roman art of fish preserving. The bass-line of most Spanish cuisine continues to be dominated by New World products: the potato, tomato, broad bean and chilli pepper. Add to this Phoenician, Greek and Jewish input and you come to realise that by tasting Spanish tapas, you taste a good part of the globe, yet the cuisine was developed long before the term 'fusion food' was coined.

In selecting tapas bars for this book, I have concentrated on places where the chefs serve evolved recipes that use relatively universal ingredients. This does not mean that you can't sample delectable tapas in Galicia, Asturias, Cantabria, Extremadura or the islands. But such regions concentrate more on local produce, such as hams and cheeses, that is rarely found outside of the regions.

So who, exactly, are these new tapas maestros? Some of the best new tapas are coming out of bars that are combined with restaurants. Most chefs remain faithful to their native regions, despite having experience of working in Madrid. Some of the chefs have trained professionally and have worked with

luminaries of the restaurant world; others are self-taught enthusiasts who have climbed the kitchen ladder. 'Grandmother's example' is often part of the equation, too, helping ensure the survival of time-honoured methods.

With tapas, the bottom line is always one of respect for the innate qualities of the ingredients, a real passion for the culinary art and a genuine desire to satisfy customers. Celebrity tapas chefs are few and far between (Catalonia and the Basque Country being exceptions as their marketing prowess comes hand-in-hand with economic acumen), partly due to that *manaña* cliché – live for today, as who knows what tomorrow will bring.

As Spanish cuisine evolves, so the rest of the world is beginning to see Hispanic produce exported along with vastly improved wines; chorizo, *jamón serrano* (literally sawn ham, but cured like all *jamón*), virgin olive oil, sherry vinegar, *bacalao* (salt cod) and *boquerónes* (pickled anchovies) can all be found worldwide. In the other direction, the Spaniards have adopted smoked salmon, pâtés, lumpfish caviar, Roquefort and cream cheese and even, in a handful of cases, started looking at Japanese sushi for tapas inspiration.

We may love Spain because it's a world apart, but globalisation marches ineluctably on. The best we can do is keep in step, follow new Hispanic trends without forgetting the best of the old, practise the *tapeo* in Spain itself and, above all, bring tapas to our homes. More than just gastronomic indulgence, some of these dishes represent cameos of the famously healthy Mediterranean diet and embody that essentially Spanish attitude to life: enjoyment of the present. Go for it! The tapas will disappear in a flash. Tomorrow is another day.

THE BASQUE REGION

María Agustina Ostiz
Baserri

Iñaki Gulin
Alex Montiel
La Cuchara de San Telmo

Josecho Marañon
Mari-Carmen Marañon
Manuel Marañon
Bar Txepetxa

Patxi Bergara
Blanca Ameztoy
Bar Bergara

*T*he road known as 'the mountain motorway' swings and dips from Navarra, through the rugged Pyrenees, before it finally descends into the Bay of Biscay. It runs through a landscape of craggy peaks, pine-forests, *caserios* (stone farmhouses with steeply pitched roofs), Alpine-style chalets, verdant meadows and the odd cluster of cows or sheep; that is, if you can see all this, as the Basque climate is characterised by *sirimiri* - a persistent drizzle that becomes the landscape. This is the road that leads to Europe's highest density of tapas bars. Your destination: San Sebastián, a 19th century resort that

trend of *nouvelle cuisine*. So it was that Spanish *nueva cocina* kicked off in the Basque country in the late 1970s, further stimulated by the region's gastronomic brotherhoods, or *txokos*. And with the recent evolution of alternative *txokos* devoted to the worship of a single product, such as potatoes from Alava or black kidney beans from Tolosa, gastronomic obsession seems unlikely to fade.

Today, the Basque region claims the world's highest concentration of gourmet restaurants per capita. Think Juan Mari Arzak, Pedro Subijana and Martín Berasategui - three gods of

'It is in the traditional seafood stakes that the Basques excel, their fleets scooping up spiny lobsters, tiny clams, squid, sea bass, red and grey mullet, scorpion fish, anchovies, tuna, sea-bream, hake, monkfish and many others.'

sweeps majestically around the bay, tucking in a fishing harbour and several hundred bars designed to transform your eating habits for ever.

Seafood is the priority here, as the Basques have always been Spain's foremost seafarers. Among them you can tick off Juan Sebastián Elcano (first to sail around the world intact) and the infamous conquistador Lope de Aguirre. Not surprisingly, the independently-minded Basques have also produced many top chefs.

The Spanish Basques' introspective culture, unique language and passion for food are shared with the French Basque region that lies a mere hop over the Pyrenees; an area that helped to accelerate the influence of the Gallic

Basque restaurant culture whose cuisines, although more formal than tapas, have influenced many of the chefs in this book. Yet there is a double face to Basque attitudes to food. Despite the accolades gained by their chefs, the population is slow to adapt to new trends – unlike the more dynamic Catalans, their closest rivals in gastronomy. This becomes apparent in the densely-packed grid of tapas bars in San Sebastián's old quarter, where innovation is hard to find. But penetrate the more upmarket, modernist Gros quarter and you'll discover innovations in the *pintxos* (Basque-style tapas) stakes.

The purely Basque *pintxo* has seen a huge renaissance in recent years, along with *la nueva cocina*. Goodbye *tortillas* and *ensaladillas*; this is Euskadi, the land of the Basques, where 'k's and 'x's pepper the language and the tapa is a gutsier version of the delicate French canapé. Discerning Basque businessmen are no longer seduced by a homemade stew made by the barman's wife, as their palates have become more finely attuned to Marinated quails with parsley oil or Smoked cod with black olive oil. The regulations for Euskadi's annual *pintxo* competitions state that it should be possible to eat a *pintxo* standing up and in a maximum of two mouthfuls. Plates and cutlery (common with tapas elsewhere in Spain) are therefore largely banished – those Basque bankers are in a hurry.

The Basques have a predilection for cider; 9,000,000 litres are downed annually in San Sebastián. A close rival is the refreshing, slightly petillant *txakoli* (white wine from Guetaria or Vizcaya) that washes down the mountains of *pintxos* adorning every bar. The Basques also boast a full-bodied red wine, Rioja Alavesa, produced in southern Euskadi on the borders of La Rioja province. Neighbouring Navarra, which shares much Basque culture, also makes increasingly acclaimed wines.

It is in the traditional seafood stakes that the Basques really excel, their fleets scooping up spiny lobsters, tiny clams, squid, sea bass, red and grey mullet, scorpion fish, anchovies, tuna, sea-bream, hake, monkfish and many others. Some Basques consider the fish caught off the Cantabrian and Basque coast to have an inimitably desirable texture due to the strong currents against which the fish must swim. Of course, there is also cod. This was first fished by Basque fishermen in the North Sea. It soon became *bacalao* (salt cod). Today, salt cod is more of an inland predilection, as the Basques opt for the fresh fish on their doorstep. But classic salt cod sauces such as green *Pil-pil* (Olive oil, garlic and parsley sauce) are so much part-and-parcel of established tastes that they are reapplied to other foods in *nueva cocina* dishes and tapas.

Another spin-off of early Basque seafarers was the range of vegetables brought from the New World. Peppers, potatoes, tomatoes, haricot beans: these were the lasting jewels in the ragged crowns of these explorers and are now cultivated from the suburbs of Bilbao (chiefly tomatoes) to the banks of the Río Ebro. Navarra harbours its own fertile swathe of market gardens bordering La Rioja. As a result, the inhabitants of the regional capital, Pamplona, when not chasing bulls, are cultivating the art of *pintxo*-sampling.

Foodie passion rears its head again in the form of mushrooms, whose prolific growth in the Pyrenean foothills has inspired specialist clubs with exhibitions, tastings and a mind-boggling range of mushroom-related activities. *Revuelta de zizak* (Scrambled egg with the first mushrooms of the season) materialises on many a bar or restaurant menu every April, while the autumn's wild *setas* are usually fried in olive oil, garlic and parsley.

From these hills, too, comes an abundance of dairy products. And the Basques are great carnivores. Superb beef, lamb, pork, game birds and other birds (thrushes among them) find their way on to the plate. The inventiveness of the new chefs is the high note to Basque cuisine, even if macho appetites monopolise the bass-line. You can follow their example in putting together unusual *pintxos*, then pile them up with Basque abandon and watch them vanish.

María Agustina Ostiz   Baserri, Pamplona

Regarded as Pamplona's most modern café-bar in the 1930s and '40s, Baserri is now a source of innovative pintxos. Hemingway himself would have slumped contentedly over a bar-stool here between bouts of bull-running. Today, the dazzling geometry of the tiled floor and bar is reminiscent of the past, yet subtlety is the mother of invention in the kitchen. Agustina – who has worked in the highly-rated Monasterio de Rocamador in Extremadura, the Hotel Castilla Plaza in Madrid, and the legendary Juan Mari Arzak and Urepel, both hallowed haunts of San Sebastián – offers an authentic taste of the Basque region. 'Navarra has a long tradition of pintxos and a strong gastronomic culture,' she says, 'so everything I make has to be of top quality. Even if the ingredients are basic, the visual aspect stimulates taste. That comes from Navarra's strong French influence.' This doesn't mean Agustina is afraid of innovation, though. 'Sometimes it's difficult to break through the traditions – I have to push people to try out new things,' she says. A range of aromatic oils for selective pintxo drizzling is new to the bar. 'In the end we must dedicate time, patience and taste,' she explains. You could say the same about savouring Baserri's pintxos. Competition is hot between Pamplona's bars, and the annual pintxos competition has seen Baserri carry off countless prizes.

Smoked salmon and curd cheese on a tomato confit
Mil hojas de tomate y queso fresco

for 8 tapas

4 large ripe tomatoes
olive oil
10g (¹/₄oz) salt
15g (¹/₂oz) thyme
1 tbsp sugar
pepper to taste
1 envelope squid ink
300ml (¹/₂ pint) sunflower oil
150g (5¹/₂oz) thinly sliced
smoked salmon
200g (7oz) queso fresco de burgos
or mozzarella, cut into 8 equal slices
4 large or 8 small anchovies in vinegar

This is Agustina's favourite *pintxo*. If squid ink is hard to find, she suggests replacing it with a gherkin vinaigrette, which is made by very finely chopping the gherkins and then treating them in the same way as the squid ink oil (below).

1 Prepare the tomato confit and the squid ink oil at least 2 hours before serving. Scald the tomatoes in boiling water for 30 seconds, then peel, halve and scoop out the insides.

2 Cut each tomato half in half again and place the pieces on a baking sheet. Drizzle with olive oil, season with salt, thyme, sugar and pepper and bake for 10 minutes at 180°C (350°F) Gas mark 4. Remove from the oven and cool.

3 Prepare the squid ink oil by blending the squid ink and sunflower oil. Heat gently, without boiling, then remove from heat and cool completely.

4 Just before serving, arrange the *pintxo* on a plate by layering 1 tomato piece, 1 slice smoked salmon, 1 slice fresh cheese, 1 (or ¹/₂, if large) anchovy and a second tomato slice for each *pintxo*. Drizzle the squid ink oil generously over the top.

Smoked cod, tomato and black olive oil toasts
(page 18)

Smoked salmon, anchovy and red pepper toasts
Pintxo de la foto

for 4 tapas
4 fresh anchovies marinated in vinegar
100g (3¹/₂oz) smoked salmon,
cut into 4 slices and rolled into
cylindrical shapes
1 red piquillo pepper (canned and
drained), cut into 4 equal parts
4 wholegrain bread rounds, toasted

for the vinaigrette
1 spring onion, finely chopped
2 red piquillo peppers or 1 ordinary red
pepper, seeded and finely chopped
1 hard-boiled egg, finely chopped
¹/₂ green pepper, seeded and
finely chopped
200ml (7fl oz) extra virgin olive oil
5 tbsp white wine vinegar

This *pintxo* was originally created for a photo shoot – hence the name '*Pintxo de la foto*'. The intention was to create a great-looking dish, but the result tasted so good that it has remained on Baserri's menu ever since. Agustina stresses the importance of the quality of the bread, as its texture is an integral part of the *pintxo*.

1 To make the vinaigrette, combine the ingredients and mix well. Set aside.

2 To prepare the *pintxo*, place the anchovies skin-side-down, and put a roll of smoked salmon in the centre of each anchovy. Fold in half and top with a piece of red *piquillo* pepper.

3 Place each anchovy roll on top of a wholegrain toast and drizzle generously with vinaigrette.

'Navarra has a long tradition of pintxos *and a strong gastronomic culture,' says Agustina,* 'so everything I make has to be of top quality.'

Smoked cod, tomato and black olive oil toasts
Bacalao ahumado y vinagreta de tomate con aceite de aceituna negra

for 8 tapas

8 slices or rounds wholegrain bread, toasted
100g (3¹/₂oz) smoked cod, thinly sliced
2 tbsp chopped chives or parsley

for the vinaigrette

1 large ripe tomato, peeled, pulp removed and finely chopped
5 tbsp extra virgin olive oil
1¹/₂ tbsp white wine vinegar
salt and pepper to taste

for the black olive oil

45g (1³/₄oz) pitted black olives, finely chopped
100ml (3¹/₂ fl oz) extra virgin olive oil

Another of Agustina's prize-winners, this *pintxo* offers a beguiling balance between the slightly sharp smoked cod and the earthy black olive oil. A spoonful of French tapenade could easily be substituted for the olives in the oil. However don't skip the wholegrain bread – Agustina says it's crucial to the balance of the dish.

1 Prepare the vinaigrette by mixing the tomato with the olive oil, white wine vinegar and seasoning.

2 Prepare the black olive oil by adding the chopped olives to the olive oil and blending well.

3 Just before serving, place 8 toasts on a serving plate and moisten each with about 1 tsp black olive oil.

4 Put a slice of smoked cod on top of the toast and dress with a heaped tbsp of vinaigrette and a little more black olive oil. Garnish with chives or parsley.

Fried courgette, prawn and bacon bundles
Rollito de calabacín con gamba y bacon

for 4 tapas

1 large courgette
4 strips lean bacon
4 prawns, cooked and peeled
salt and pepper to taste
1 beaten egg for coating
flour for coating
olive oil for frying
4 sesame seed toasts or crackers

This *pintxo* is quite fiddly to prepare, but once you have mastered the technique you will use it again and again.

1 Cut the courgette in half lengthways, then cut 4 x 3mm (¹/₈-inch) slices, again lengthways, from one of the halves.

2 On each slice lay 1 strip of bacon and place 1 prawn on the end, then season with salt and pepper.

3 Roll the courgette up, being careful to ensure that the prawn stays in the centre, and secure with a toothpick.

4 Carefully dip the bundle in egg and then flour. Heat about 3cm (1¹/₄ inches) olive oil in a frying pan and cook the rolls until golden. Drain on a paper towel.

5 Serve promptly on a sesame seed toast or cracker.

Iñaki Gulin, Alex Montiel   La Cuchara de San Telmo, San Sebastián

Tucked away in the shadow of San Telmo on San Sebastián's narrowest street is a rock and roll altar to Basque nueva cocina - La Cuchara de San Telmo. Through the flickering flames and clouds of steam in the kitchen, you can just about make out the toiling figures of Iñaki Gulin and Alex Montiel. These two young chefs combine culinary traditions from their native Basque and Catalonia (respectively) with training in top restaurants and a good dose of inventiveness. Ask them where their inspiration comes from, though, and they cite their mothers Celia and María-Carmen, both professional cooks. 'Cooks are the soul of a house,' says Iñaki, 'and you need to follow their example by making things with hope and affection.'

Iñaki and Alex set out to create restaurant-quality food that can be consumed at the bar, on the hoof and at minimal cost. As a result, the tapas are innovative and often elaborate. 'We change the menu every two to three months according to the season, but we can't change everything; we must consider our more traditional customers,' says Iñaki. 'We may take a classic dish and bring it up to date through presentation or by adding extra ingredients. But in the end people should be able to trust you and eat with their eyes closed.' The best option at La Cuchara, however, is to keep your eyes wide open - so as not to miss out on the next offering.

Marinated quail with apple purée and parsley oil
Cordoniz en escabeche de Modena

for 8 tapas
3 tart apples, such as Granny Smiths
4 quails, cleaned, halved and splayed
salt and pepper to taste
olive oil for frying
6 tbsp sunflower oil, plus 1 more tbsp
for frying
2¹/2 tbsp balsamic vinegar, plus a
little extra for sprinkling
2 medium courgettes, thinly sliced
50ml (2fl oz) beef broth
100ml (3¹/2fl oz) parsley oil

for the parsley oil
2 cloves garlic
leaves from a small bunch of parsley
100g (3¹/2oz) walnuts, shelled
200ml (7fl oz) sunflower oil
salt to taste

This dish looks luxuriously juicy – and it is, with the quail's bountiful coating of marinade and its bed of slightly tart apple purée. The quantities here give you more parsley oil than you need for this recipe, but it's difficult to make it in very small quantities, so use it for other tapas or *pintxos*.

1 First make the parsley oil. Blend the garlic, parsley and nuts in a mini-blender or small food processor. Slowly add the oil, with the motor still running. Add salt to taste. Set aside.

2 To prepare the apple purée, wash, quarter and core the apples. Partially cover with water and simmer for about 30 minutes, until soft. Put through a food mill or blender, skin and all.

3 1 hour before serving, season the quails and brown them in olive oil for 2 minutes on each side. In a small pan, heat the sunflower oil and vinegar. Add the quails, cover, and cook slowly for 20 minutes, turning the quails.

4 While the quails are cooking, quickly sauté the courgette slices on both sides in 1 tbsp of hot sunflower oil. As soon as they are tender, sprinkle with vinegar and quickly reduce the liquid. Set aside.

5 Spoon some apple purée on to 8 plates, place a quail half on top, and lay a few courgette slices over it. Splash with beef broth, then drizzle with a little of the oil and vinegar in which you cooked the quail. Drizzle on some parsley oil.

Tomato stuffed with tuna, garlic and parsley
Tomate relleno de ventresca de bonito

for 4 tapas

*150g (5¹/₂oz) tuna belly, lightly
cooked in oil (or canned white tuna)
2¹/₂ tbsp parsley oil (see page 21)
4 large, firm tomatoes
4 tbsp sunflower oil
1¹/₂ tbsp balsamic vinegar*

for the tomato sauce

*1 x 400g tin tomatoes in thick juice
¹/₂ onion, finely chopped
1 stick celery, finely chopped
3 cloves garlic, sliced
1 tbsp tomato purée
3 tbsp olive oil
¹/₂ tbsp caster sugar*

for the alioli

*1 clove garlic, crushed
1 egg
100ml (3¹/₂fl oz) sunflower oil
lemon juice to taste
a little milk*

This dish offers an unusual combination of flavours and textures – the rich tuna, fresh tomato and pungent garlic are all complemented by the parsley oil. These tomatoes should be eaten at room temperature. The recipe for tomato sauce makes more than you need, but keep it in the fridge for other tapas or pasta.

1 To make the tomato sauce, put all the ingredients for it into a saucepan and bring to the boil. Turn down to a simmer and cook for half an hour, until it is thick and jammy. Check the seasoning, and purée.

2 To make the *alioli*, mix the garlic and egg in a small blender, then slowly add the sunflower oil, a little at a time, until the mixture is thick and creamy. Add lemon juice and salt and pepper to taste.

3 About 1 hour before serving, prepare the tuna stuffing by combining in a blender the tuna, 2¹/₂ tbsp of the tomato sauce, 2 tbsp of alioli, 1½ tbsp of parsley oil, salt and pepper. Blend until thick and creamy. Set aside.

4 About half an hour before serving, blanch, peel and halve the tomatoes and scoop out the insides. Fill each one with the tuna stuffing and place it upside down on a serving plate.

5 To make the vinaigrette, whisk the oil and vinegar together with seasoning until well blended. Drizzle the tomatoes with the remaining parsley oil and then with vinaigrette. Add a little milk to the remaining *alioli* to thin it and pour a thin stream of this over the whole dish.

Savoury millefeuilles
El Cremat

for 6 tapas

*6 onions, finely chopped
6 tbsp olive oil for frying
6 slices bacon, in small pieces, sautéed
100ml (3¹/₂fl oz) double cream
salt and pepper to taste
2 green apples, peeled and thinly
sliced, with the slices covered
in lemon juice
200g (7oz) duck pâté
100g (3¹/₂oz) smoked eel, in thin strips
sugar for caramelising*

There is a mantra (see the layering order below) behind the preparation of this wondrous dish that you will probably be chanting in your sleep once you've savoured the tapa. This is a work of gastronomic art, with the addition of the caramelised sugar being the finishing touch that spells *nueva cocina*.

1 At least 8 hours before serving, sauté the onions in the oil without colouring them. Turn the heat down very low, cover, and cook for about 1½ hours. Make sure the onions don't 'catch' at the bottom by adding ¹/₂ tbsp water a few times during the cooking. The onions will be soft and caramelised. Remove excess oil and add the bacon and cream. Cook to reduce the cream right down, then season. Remove from the heat and set aside to cool.

2 Arrange all the ingredients in thin layers in a shallow rectangular baking dish in the following order: apple, pâté, apple, pâté, apple, onion, apple, eel, apple, onion, apple, pâté, apple, pâté, apple. Press down after the addition of each layer. Refrigerate for at least 6 hours.

3 Unmould the dish and cut into squares. Dust each portion with sugar and caramelise it with the use of a blow torch or run it quickly under the grill.

FOIE SALTEADO CON OREJONES
BACALAO AL PIL-PIL DE PEREJIL
RAVIOLI DE BACON Y ESPINACA
BERTSOLI DE ANTXOA
CODORNIZ ESCABECHADA
TOSTA DE CALLOS AL ALL i OLI
CANELON CREMOSO DE MORCILLA
TXIPIRON RELLENO DE CEBOLLETA
CREMA FRIA DE BACALAO CON TOMATE
MAGRET ASADO CON MANZANA
RISOTTO DE MORCILLA
MORROS ASADOS CON VINAGRETA
TOMATE RELLENO DE MENDRESKA
CARRILLERA GUISADA AL VINO TINTO
ENTRECOT DE BUEY (RACION)
TXOKOLATE CON NARANJA CONFITADA
SOPA DE YOGUR CON MANZANA

Josecho Marañon
Mari-Carmen Marañon
Manuel Marañon Bar Txepetxa, San Sebastián

When you tire of the fantasy-laden baguette slices that monopolise many of San Sebastián's pintxos bars, Bar Txepetxa will spell salvation. At the heart of the pintxos from this 30-year-old family business are succulent, silvery anchovies, marinated according to a recipe by Josecho Marañon, prepared by his wife Mari-Carmen and served by their son Manuel, who insists: 'Our success lies in the hands of my mother and the palate of my father.'

The small bar, plastered with photos and the odd gastronomic distinction (including a certificate of honour from San Sebastián's Anchovy Brotherhood), is packed with drinkers enjoying these anchovies with 15 accompaniments. Each one, whether coconut, papaya, herrings' eggs, liver or sea-urchins' eggs, is laid between the fat silver sheaths with almost sushi-style precision. What regulars avoid is the platter of plastic models, so perfect that unsuspecting newcomers reach out to help themselves. Foiled! This highlights one of the reasons for Txepetxa's popularity: the fact that every pintxo is freshly prepared. 'I wanted to give people who came from the hills something from the sea,' explains Josecho. 'They need to taste the salt water as well as see it.' Sadly, Josecho won't reveal the recipe for his marinade, but these pintxos taste great with anchovies simply marinated in vinegar.

Anchovy and trout caviar toasts
Anchoa con huevos de trucha

for 4 tapas
8 anchovy fillets marinated in vinegar
4 slices French bread, freshly toasted
4 tsp trout eggs

This classic Josecho Marañon recipe is a favourite among customers at Bar Txepetxa and it is simple to make at home.

1 For each *pintxo*, lay 2 anchovy fillets on a slice of freshly toasted French bread.

2 Place 1 tsp trout eggs in a line down the middle of each toast. Serve immediately.

Anchovy and vegetable toasts
Anchoa jardinera

for 4 tapas
1 small green pepper, finely chopped
1 small red pepper, finely chopped
1 small onion, finely chopped
2 cloves garlic, finely chopped
1 chilli pepper, halved, seeded and finely chopped
leaves from a small bunch of fresh parsley, finely chopped
3 tbsp sunflower oil
8 anchovy fillets marinated in vinegar
4 slices French bread, freshly toasted

This deliciously fresh *pintxo* takes pride of place on a plate of mixed anchovy toasts, adding a splash of colour and a crisp texture.

1 Marinate the vegetables and herbs in the sunflower oil for half an hour to prevent them from drying out and to leave them glistening.

2 For each *pintxo*, lay 2 anchovy fillets on a slice of freshly toasted French bread. Spoon some of the marinated vegetables on top of the anchovies. Serve immediately.

Anchovy and smoked salmon toasts
Anchoa salmón ahumado

for 4 tapas
8 anchovy fillets marinated in vinegar
4 slices French bread, freshly toasted
2 slices smoked salmon, cut into strips

A simple, subtle yet extravagant-tasting *pintxo*. Use the best smoked salmon you can find.

1 For each *pintxo*, lay 2 anchovy fillets on a slice of freshly toasted French bread.

2 Top each toast with a little mound of smoked salmon strips. Serve immediately.

Anchovy and crab toasts
Lomos de anchoa con crema de centolla

for 4 tapas
meat of 1 cooked crab, finely chopped
2 lettuce leaves, finely shredded
1 hard-boiled egg, chopped
2 tbsp mayonnaise
2 tsp lemon juice
8 anchovy fillets marinated in vinegar
4 slices French bread, freshly toasted

A real taste of the sea! If you prefer a meatier flavour, do what Josecho does and add a slice of finely chopped cooked ham to the crab mixture.

1 Mix the crab, lettuce and egg together. Stir in the mayonnaise and lemon juice.

2 For each *pintxo*, lay 2 anchovy fillets on a slice of freshly toasted French bread, then cover with the crab mixture. Serve immediately.

Anchovy, tapenade and onion toasts
Lomos de anchoa con pâté de olivas

for 4 tapas
1 small onion, finely chopped
2 tbsp lemon juice
8 anchovy fillets marinated in vinegar
4 slices French bread, freshly toasted
3 tbsp tapenade

An intense-tasting *pintxo* - the one none of your guests will be able to forget! Delicious as an appetiser.

1 Marinate the onion in the lemon juice for at least 2 hours.

2 For each *pintxo*, put 2 anchovy fillets on a slice of freshly toasted slice of French bread, cover with 2 tsp of tapenade, then sprinkle with the chopped onion. Serve immediately.

Patxi Bergara, Blanca Ameztoy Bar Bergara, San Sebastián

Since Patxi Bergara and his wife Blanca Ameztoy took over the family bar 15 years ago, it has leapt up San Sebastián's pintxo charts, reaping prizes for its adventurous yet subtle flavour combinations and sophisticated presentation. All the dishes meet the pintxo criteria of being consumable in two mouthfuls, but the problem is where and when to finish, for the bar is laid out like a banquet.

Not surprisingly for the Basque port and resort of San Sebastián, seafood features prominently, with pintxos such as King prawns fried with mushrooms and Bacalao mixed with ratatouille and potato mousse, and a strong focus on the king of pintxo ingredients, the anchovy. Hardly surprising, then, that Bar Bergara has been chosen to represent San Sebastián at overseas functions and to fill the bellies of the finalists of the Tour de France or those of the stars at the annual film festival. The bar runs like clockwork, with Patxi filling glasses from his vast selection of wines and Blanca heading up the kitchen.

Bar Bergara may have been around for more than 50 years but, because of the talent and enterprise of its owners, its shelf-life is far from over.

Pork, pepper and melted cheese toasts
Montadito

for 4 tapas

4 thin slices pork loin fillet, about 50g (1 3/4oz) each
1 green pepper, quartered and seeded
olive oil
salt and pepper
4 slices French bread, lightly toasted
4 thin slices creamy, easy-melting cheese such as French Chaumes, about 30g (1 1/4oz) each

This wonderfully simple *pintxo* is comfort food at its best, with its satisfying combination of pork, cheese and bread.

1 Brush the pork and pepper with olive oil and season the pork with salt and pepper. On a hot griddle, cook the pork and pepper until the pork is cooked through and the pepper is soft. Set them aside.

2 Place the French bread toasts on a baking sheet. Top each piece with a loin fillet, a green pepper quarter and a slice of cheese. Place under a very hot grill for about 30 seconds. Remove from the grill and serve immediately.

Scrambled eggs with anchovy and red pepper on toast
Revuelto de anchoas con piquillos

for 4 tapas

100g (3 1/2oz) fresh anchovies
1 clove garlic, minced
olive oil for frying
1 small tin (about 100g/3 1/2oz) red piquillo peppers, drained and cut into thin strips
2 eggs, beaten
4 thin slices French bread, toasted
1 small green pepper, cut into thin strips and quickly fried

This dish looks fabulous, but if you prefer a more sophisticated *pintxo*, use a small pastry case instead of toast and heat it, with the filling, under the grill at the last minute. If you can't get fresh anchovies, use those marinated in vinegar, but drain them and cover in olive oil for a couple of hours before using.

1 Sauté the anchovies and garlic in a little olive oil. (If using marinated anchovies, sauté the garlic on its own, then add the anchovies and gently heat through.) Add the red peppers and eggs and stir until all the ingredients are mixed and the eggs are just set.

2 Immediately spread the mixture on the toasts and garnish with a grid of green pepper strips.

Blue cheese and anchovy tartlets
Hojaldre relleno

for 8 tapas
50g (1³/4oz) Roquefort or other soft
blue cheese, crumbled
200ml (7fl oz) double cream, whipped
4 anchovy fillets in oil, drained
and halved

for the 8 tartlet cases
200g (7oz) plain flour, plus extra
for rolling
¹/2 tsp salt
90g (3¹/4oz) butter, softened
2 small egg yolks

Hidden between the pastry cases lies a rich, flavoursome filling, so be sure to serve this *pintxo* with a refreshing white wine. Txakoli, the Basque favourite, is ideal, but in its absence look for a light, dry sparkling white.

1 To make the pastry, put the flour, salt and butter in a food processor and process with the pastry blade until the mixture resembles fine breadcrumbs. Add the egg yolks mixed with a bit of cold water a little at a time, continuing to blend. Just add enough to make the pastry come together in a ball. Wrap in cling-film and refrigerate for half an hour.

2 Roll the pastry out on a floured surface and cut it into shapes to fit 8 tartlet tins. Also cut out some 'lids'. Prick the bottoms of the tartlets and chill for 20 minutes. Fill the tartlets with a few dried beans so that they can bake blind. Put the lids on a baking sheet and cook both cases and lids in an oven

pre-heated to 200°C (400°F) Gas mark 6 for about 15 minutes or until pale gold in colour. Cool in the tins.

3 For the filling, blend the cheese and the whipped cream with a wooden spoon until smooth. Set aside.

4 Remove the tartlet cases from their tins and place ¹/2 an anchovy on the bottom of each one. Fill the pastry shells with the cheese and cream mixture and top with the pastry lid.

5 Place the pastries on a baking sheet and heat in a hot oven at 220°C (425°F) Gas mark 7 for 1 minute. Remove from the oven and serve.

Mushroom, prawn and cheese tartlets
Txalupa

for 8 tapas
100g (3¹/2oz) mushrooms, chopped
2 cloves garlic, finely minced
30g (1oz) butter
salt to taste
125ml (4fl oz) sparkling white wine
125ml (4fl oz) double cream
10 large prawns, peeled
and chopped
125g (4¹/2oz) queso Ibérico or
mature Cheddar cheese, grated

for the 8 tartlet cases
100g (3¹/2oz) plain flour, plus extra
for rolling
¹/4 tsp salt
40g (1¹/2oz) butter, softened
1 small egg yolk

Typically subtle in flavour, this *pintxo* also looks the part. Again, be sure to serve this with a refreshing white wine.

1 Make the pastry and prepare and cook the pastry cases according to points 1 and 2 in the recipe above, but omitting the pastry lids.

2 To make the filling, sauté the mushrooms and garlic in butter over a low heat for 20 minutes. Sprinkle on salt to taste, add the white wine, bring to the boil and reduce until there is barely any liquid left. Add the cream and prawns and continue to cook for 3 minutes, stirring occasionally. Remove from the heat.

3 Remove the pastry shells from their tins. Scoop the mixture into them and top with grated cheese. Place under the grill for 2 minutes, until the cheese is golden. Serve immediately.

CATALONIA

Carlos Abellan
Comerç24

Albert Asin
Bar Pinotxo

Paco Guzman
Santa María

Josep Manubens
Cal Pep

*T*he words 'tapas' and 'Catalonia' don't always mix, but 'tapas' and 'Barcelona' certainly do. Although the Catalans have never embraced the tapa as single-mindedly as other inhabitants of Spain have, Barcelona is now transforming the habit in typically perfectionist style. This city, an enclave of Catalan culture entwined with Gallic influences, is a world apart from the rest of Spain. These influences are reflected in the Catalan language, a unique though not impenetrable blend of Provençal French and Castilian Spanish. Dynamic and forward-looking, with a strong mercantile streak,

gastronomic temple, El Bulli, reigns supreme over the rocky Costa Brava. Adrià's influence has spawned clones throughout this elegant city and well beyond, adding touches of fusion cuisine to Catalonia's vast range of home-grown products.

Eat at El Bulli and you will be confronted with dishes of Miró-esque composition and colour, such as Mango ravioli flanked by basil jelly and an orange-ginger confit, a far cry from *Pa amb tomaquet* (Bread rubbed with juicy tomatoes and seasoned with salt and olive oil), the basic but delicious snack that is eaten by Catalan workmen.

'Designer bars dominate as nowhere else in Spain. Inside their customers imbibe the sparkling wine cava, or still wines, both red and white, from the wine regions of Penedès or Priorato, while indulging in tapas that reach new heights of inventiveness.'

Barcelona has reinvented itself, since hosting the 1992 Olympics, into a cultural powerhouse and gastronomic capital, adding further layers to its already rich past. Designer bars dominate as nowhere else in Spain. Inside their customers imbibe the sparkling wine known as *cava* or still wines, both white and red, from the wine regions of Penedès or Priorato, while indulging in tapas and *raciones* that reach new heights of inventiveness.

See Barcelona and think Gaudí – it's impossible to miss his surrealistic, *modernista* flights of fantasy, including the still unfinished spires of the Sagrada Famìlia temple. Taste Barcelona and think Ferran Adrià, the polemical pioneer of new Catalan cuisine, whose

Although Adrià does not serve tapas, his disciples – including Carlos Abellan of Comerç24 – do.

Catalan gastronomic history is markedly different from that of the rest of the peninsula. It was on the Costa Brava that the first foreign seeds were sown, with Roman settlements holding sway for more than six centuries. From them, the Catalans inherited large-scale fish salting, the predecessor of L'Escala's anchovy preserves, which are still rated as the best in Spain. The Moorish occupation, though short-lived, introduced foods such as aubergines, saffron and spinach, which remain influential in Catalan cooking today. Intrepid French monks, Benedictines and Cistercians followed, who not only built extraordinary medieval monasteries such as Montserrat, but also cultivated grapes when not saving souls. The Italian influence returned in the 15th century, when Catalonia united with the Kingdom of Naples and Sicily. The fast-developing cuisine now had the first Catalan cookbooks: the *Libre de Sent Soví* and the *Libre del Coch*. The Gallic input, which was first brought by Charlemagne's army back in the 9th century, and long reinforced by Catalonia's geographic proximity to France, has left a notable impression on the region's taste-buds.

Catalan *bourgeois* cuisine is known for its sauces. Many of these are based on the *Sofregit*, which is composed of a typically Mediterranean blend of olive oil, onion, garlic and tomato – all ingredients that are used again and again in tapas. *Alioli*, whether cold or warm, crowns many a tapa with its garlic-flavoured trickle of mayonnaise. Like the French and Italians, and unlike the Castilians and Basques, the Catalans revel in aromatic herbs: fennel, bay leaf, parsley, thyme, mint and juniper berries. Chocolate (added to game dishes), cinnamon (flavouring pastas or pork belly) and saffron play the jokers in the seasoning pack, providing further confirmation that Catalonia really does have a mind of its own – gastronomically, culturally and indeed economically.

Mar i montaña (literally 'sea and mountains'): this defines not only a typically Catalan combination of ingredients, such as clams with ham or bacon with squid, but also the extremes of the region's topographic identity. Although Catalonia is strongly industrialised, its diverse landscape ranges from the dramatic cliffs of the coastline to wide valleys, plains, lakes, fast-flowing rivers, a huge delta, a limestone sierra to the south and the green Pyrenees to the north. Put together, this network of micro-climates ensures virtual self-sufficiency in nutritional terms. Go to Barcelona's teeming Bouquería market and you can pack your basket with goat's, cow's and sheep's milk cheeses, lamb and wild mushrooms from the Pyrenees, tomatoes, olive oils, watermelons, peaches, grapes, apricots and figs, Mediterranean fish and shellfish, *embutidos* (sausages) and hams from the Gerona area and pulses from the volcanoes of Olot. The latter, a vast swathe of dormant craters that is blanketed with fertile cropland and pastures, produces a range of 'volcanic' organic food, some of which you can find incorporated into Barcelona's tastiest tapas.

Outside the market, Las Ramblas – Barcelona's heady main thoroughfare (actually five connected streets) – slices down to the harbour, source of the city's abundant Mediterranean seafood. Beyond lie the narrow, laundry-strung streets of the Barri Gòtic (Gothic Quarter), the towering cathedral, a chunk of Roman wall and a medieval palace courtyard. With a nod to the Picasso Museum, cross yourself at Santa María del Mar, the seamen's church, then plunge into the hip Born district, tucked behind Barceloneta ('Little Barcelona') and the new marina. Here the city's funkiest young designers promote their wares; it is also where some of the most innovative cuisine is produced. Eixample, the elegant grid of early 19th century Barcelona, may boast architectural jewels, but it is Born that nurtures fantasy. So when you tuck into the tapas in this chapter, take time to savour the inspiration. You may find yourself fizzing with new ideas.

Carlos Abellan   Comerç24, Barcelona

Suave yet wickedly ironic, Carlos Abellan is driven by the pleasure of sharing food with friends. 'Tapas is about how you eat food,' he says, 'it's about small portions and sharing.' He wanted to put tapas in a restaurant environment at Comerç24, and it certainly does offer an ultra-sophisticated setting, despite Carlos' insistence that 'you can feel relaxed here.' At the long bar customers perch on upholstered bar chairs to consume nueva cocina tapas that range from modern dishes such as Basil salmorejo with lychees to traditional ones such as Tripe with houmous.

Carlos flies the flag of his mentor Ferran Adriá, with whom he worked before moving on to Talaia Mar in Barcelona's Olympic Village. He subsequently spent two years commuting to Seville to scout for and set up Adriá's Andalucian outpost, Hacienda Benacuza. 'I spent so much time in airports and on planes that I started devising ideas for my own place,' explains Carlos. 'It took root in this area, purely by chance, when I came to see friends here.' Comerç24 opened its doors in summer 2001.

Carlos is adamant that he's not trying to do 'creative' cuisine. But while he may express immunity to gastronomic fantasies, his customers certainly don't.

Catalan grilled fish with broth
Suquet de Pescado

for 4 tapas
olive oil
2 cloves garlic, crushed
2 tbsp fresh chopped parsley
*2 tomatoes, peeled, seeded
and chopped*
1 litre (1³/4 pints) fish stock
*4 medium-sized new potatoes,
peeled and diced*
1/2 tsp sweet Spanish paprika
salt and pepper to taste
4 x 175g (6oz) fish fillets, such as hake

This Catalan classic goes well beyond the quantity boundaries of tapas, so it can move up your menu to slot in as a first or second course. At Comerç24 it is served with purées of aubergine and potatoes, which are both good for soaking up the ambrosial fish juices.

1 Using a little olive oil, sauté the garlic in a large frying pan until tender but not browned. Add the parsley and tomatoes and cook over a low heat, stirring, until the mixture thickens.

2 Add the fish stock, potatoes and paprika to the tomatoes and cook for about 10 minutes, or until the potatoes are tender. Season the dish with salt and pepper

3 While the broth is cooking, grill the fish fillets, skin-side down, until golden. Serve the fish broth at once in bowls, with the fish fillets on the side.

Marinated tuna cubes
Bonito en sashimi marinado

for 4 tapas
50ml (2fl oz) soy sauce
50ml (2fl oz) sunflower oil
150g (5¹/₂oz) fresh tuna, cut into
3cm (1¹/₄-inch) cubes
2 tbsp sesame seeds
soy oil

Carlos Abellan serves this tapa in a porcelain dish specially designed for such cubes, but the food's so stylish it would look good on almost anything. Make sure the tuna is ultra-fresh, as this is the heart of the dish. For an even more intense flavour, lightly sprinkle some powdered ginger or some grated fresh ginger over the cubes.

1 Prepare the marinade by mixing the soy sauce and sunflower oil together. Add the tuna and leave it to marinate for at least 12 hours.

2 Thread the tuna cubes on skewers. Top each cube with a sprinkling of sesame seeds and drizzle with a little soy oil. Serve promptly.

'Tapas is about the form of food and about how you eat it; it's about small portions and sharing...'

Bacon-squid bundles with squid ink vinaigrette
Ataditos de calamar con vinagreta de tinta

for 4 tapas
8 slices cured bacon
1 large squid, cleaned, prepared
and cut into fine julienne
olive oil for frying
1 tsp squid ink
100ml (3¹/₂fl oz) sunflower oil

This unusual combination of flavours, with its squid and bacon, is another typical Catalan application of the *mar y montaña* (sea and mountain) theme.

1 Cut each slice of bacon in two lengthways. Wrap thin strips of bacon around the middle of bunches of julienned squid to form little bundles and then fix with toothpicks.

2 Sauté the bundles in a little oil on a medium heat until the bacon is crisp. Drain on kitchen paper and transfer to a serving plate.

3 Make the vinaigrette by mixing the squid ink with the sunflower oil. Drizzle over the bundles. Serve immediately.

Roasted tomatoes with fresh cheese and anchovies
Requesón con tomate y anchoas con vinagreta de garúm

for 8 tapas

8 ripe tomatoes, peeled, seeded and halved
olive oil for drizzling
salt to taste
caster sugar to taste
2¹/₂ tbsp extra virgin olive oil
1¹/₂ tsp black olive tapenade
1 small bunch fresh basil, finely chopped
200g (7oz) fresh requesón or ricotta cheese
16 anchovy fillets, drained of oil
20g (³/₄oz) pine nuts, fried in olive oil

for the Parmesan crisps (optional)

500g (1lb 2oz) Parmesan, grated
20g (³/₄oz) butter

Choose requesón for your fresh cheese – it's the Spanish equivalent of ricotta. It provides the perfect subtle backdrop for the intense flavours of the anchovies, tomatoes and basil and olive vinaigrette.

1 Place the tomatoes on a baking sheet. Drizzle with olive oil, sprinkle with a little salt and sugar, and bake at 150ºC (300ºF) Gas mark 1 for 30 minutes. Remove from the oven and cool.

2 If you're going to garnish the dish with Parmesan crisps, melt the butter in a frying pan and spoon on pancake shapes of cheese (about 3 tbsp for each crisp). Press the cheese down and fry on each side until golden. Remove and set on kitchen paper.

3 Prepare a vinaigrette by blending the extra virgin olive oil with the black olive tapenade and the finely chopped basil.

4 Arrange the tomatoes on a plate. Mound the cheese on top of each half, then lay an anchovy over this. Sprinkle with pine nuts, drizzle with vinaigrette, and top with Parmesan crisps if using.

Albert Asin   Bar Pinotxo, Barcelona

Bar Pinotxo has been preparing a feast of tapas for its faithful clientele for 60 years. The stoves are now in the hands of Albert Asin, one of the five members of the Bayen family who squeeze in and out of the bar-kitchen in the heart of the Boquería market. Watching him work in his galley-kitchen is like watching a miracle in the making, as huge pans and woks are shifted around the stove in clouds of steam, with earthenware dishes piled above and ingredients somehow squeezed in below, all just inches away from waiting customers.

'My greatest innovation has been the wok,' says Albert, 'a friend brought one in and I haven't been without it since. It's the world's oldest cooking utensil – and the best!' The wok aside, Albert is a self-confessed traditionalist. But he is not afraid of progress: 'This location means I can find the best products in the market and improve the basic recipes accordingly,' he says. 'Good oil and salt, for example, make a huge difference.'

Before Albert took over the cooking at Bar Pinotxo it was done by his mother María, and before that by his grandfather Juan. Albert's father incarnates unofficial customer-relations status, while brother Jordi and sister-in-law Titi transport the fare to market stallholders.

Chickpeas with black pudding in garlic and parsley
Garbanzos con butifarra negra

for 4 tapas
olive oil
1/2 large onion, thinly sliced
1 clove garlic, finely chopped
2 tbsp finely chopped fresh parsley
25g (1oz) sultanas, soaked in hot water for 15 minutes and drained
10g (1/4oz) pine nuts
150g (51/2oz) black pudding, fried and coarsely chopped
1 x 400g can cooked chickpeas, drained and rinsed
salt and pepper to taste

This classic Catalan tapa is a wonderful blend of creamy chickpeas, sweet sultanas, meaty black pudding and crunchy pine nuts; a truly Hispanic assault on the senses!

1 Put 2 tbsp olive oil in a saucepan over a low heat, then sauté the onion until it is just tender. Add the garlic, parsley, sultanas and pine nuts and mix.

2 Add the black pudding and chickpeas and heat through, stirring all the time. Season with salt and pepper. Transfer to a serving platter, drizzle with olive oil and serve at once.

47

Sardines marinated in chilli, garlic and bay leaves
Sardinas en escabeche

for 6 tapas
12 fresh medium sardines, scaled
and gutted
flour for coating
100ml (3¹/₂fl oz) olive oil
pepper to taste
1 dried red chilli pepper, minced
12 cloves garlic
1 tbsp sweet Spanish paprika
3 bay leaves
100ml (3¹/₂fl oz) white wine vinegar
100ml (3¹/₂fl oz) dry white wine
100ml (3¹/₂fl oz) water
salt to taste

Simple, grilled sardines are ubiquitous throughout Spain, but Albert's marinade transforms them into an aromatic sensation. While this tapa is explicitly garlicky, the slight bitterness of the bay leaves gives it a cutting edge. It tastes even better a day later.

1 At least 2¹/₂ hours before serving, coat the sardines lightly with flour on both sides and quickly fry in hot oil to brown each side. Place in a shallow earthenware dish.

2 Strain the oil that was used to fry the sardines and, when cool, return it to the frying pan and add the pepper, chilli pepper and garlic. Fry gently until the garlic is golden.

3 Remove from the heat and add the paprika, bay leaves, vinegar, wine, water and salt to the pan. Bring to the boil and boil for 1 minute.

4 Pour the hot liquid over the sardines and leave to marinate at room temperature for at least 2 hours.

5 These sardines can be served hot, cold or at room temperature.

'What I prepare is mainly traditional, but this location means that I can find the best products in the market, and improve the basic recipes accordingly.'

White beans with cuttlefish in garlic and parsley
Mongetes de Santa Pau con chipirones

for 8 tapas
3 tbsp olive oil
400g (14oz) fresh cuttlefish, prepared
and cleaned
1 clove garlic, minced
salt and pepper to taste
250g (9oz) white beans, cooked
and drained
2 tbsp finely chopped flat-leaf parsely
balsamic vinegar

White beans from Santa Pau will make your tapa truly Catalan, but if you can't get them, substitute other beans. Choose ones that are as small as possible; even canned beans are fine. Equally, the cuttlefish can be replaced by squid.

1 Heat the oil in a wok or a frying pan over a high heat and add the cuttlefish, garlic and a little pepper. Sauté for 1 minute, tossing the fish and garlic.

2 Add the white beans and parsley and continue to sauté for 1 more minute. Season with salt and pepper. Transfer to a serving platter, splash with vinegar and serve immediately.

Paco Guzman   Santa María, Barcelona

Paco Guzman is a man on the move. Now you see him, now you don't. When visible, he is a blur behind the glass screen that separates his kitchen from his low-tech bar and restaurant; when invisible, he is on his bike scouring the Boquería market for ingredients, visiting organic suppliers or checking out his other designer restaurant, Convent dels Angels.

Paco's Basque and Riojan origins, when combined with his culinary training in France, may give him a head start in creativity, but the greatest influences on his gastronomic style have been his Asian globe-trotting and time spent as a chef in Tokyo. Ever alert to what's in season and what's healthy, Paco's tapas menu changes regularly, and each new list – clipped to translucent lampshades above the bar – offers a sumptuous juxtaposition of ingredients.

'I decided to open an informal restaurant in which small portions of top-quality food meant that anyone could enjoy the dishes,' explains Paco. Packed in the evening, quieter at lunchtimes, Santa María has rapidly become a gastronomic landmark since it opened in 1999. It's easy to understand this when you hear Paco describe his passion for cooking: 'Mixing flavours is like playing a piano of sensations – pressing different keys brings out tastes, textures, aromas and nutritional balance.' That elusive eastern balance has arrived in Barcelona.

Pumpkin, chestnut, feta cheese and pomegranate salad
Ensalada de calabaza, castañas y queso feta

for 8 tapas

Leaves from half an oakleaf lettuce or 175g lamb's lettuce, torn into bite-sized pieces
1 small curly endive (frisée) lettuce, coarse leaves removed and torn into bite-sized pieces
1 bunch watercress
225g (8oz) feta cheese, broken into small cubes
1¹/2 spring onions, thinly sliced
seeds of 1 pomegranate
200g (7oz) chestnuts, cooked, peeled and halved
350g (12oz) pumpkin flesh, cut into fine julienne
2 tbsp white wine vinegar
6 tbsp extra virgin olive oil
salt and pepper to taste

The happy collusion between Paco Guzman's Asian influences and Catalonia's fantastic array of autumnal produce has inspired this salad tapa. Every autumn, chestnut-roasters take root in the streets of Spain, while market stalls acquire the Dali-esque shapes and colours of abundant squash varieties. In this recipe, you can vary or simplify the lettuce types, as the main interest lies in the balance of fresh pumpkin, chestnuts, feta and sweet pomegranate seeds.

1 Arrange all the salad ingredients in 8 individual bowls or 1 large one.

2 Make the vinaigrette by whisking the white wine vinegar and olive oil together and seasoning with the salt and pepper.

3 Dress the salad lightly, toss thoroughly, and serve immediately.

Duck's liver with sweet pears and Szechuan pepper
Higado de pato con pera y pimiento Szechuan

for 4 tapas
60g (2¹/₄oz) sugar
5 tbsp water
2 pears, peeled and thinly sliced
150g (5¹/₂oz) duck's liver, cut into 4 slices
1 tbsp olive oil
4 tsp Szechuan pepper

Duck's liver is the creamiest, smoothest liver you can get, and in Paco Guzman's recipe it is perfectly combined with fresh poached pear and a hint of mild Szechuan pepper – although you can use chicken's liver if duck's liver isn't available. This is a rich tapa and you won't need second helpings!

1 Mix the sugar and water in a pan and heat until the sugar has dissolved. Add the pears and poach until it is just tender. Drain the pears, reserving the liquid, and set the fruit aside. Bring the liquid to the boil and boil until syrupy. Return the pears to the liquid and mix well.

2 Sauté the liver in the oil until it is lightly browned on each side. Arrange on a plate.

3 Spoon some pear and syrup beside each liver slice. Grind the pepper and alogside. Serve immediately.

'Mixing flavours is like playing a piano of sensations – pressing different keys brings out tastes, textures, aromas and nutritional balance.'

Santa María # 65

- Chips de yuca 375
- Anchoas con pan con tomate 675
- Mojama de atún con cebolla tierna y aceite de oliva 675
- Cecina de león 775
- Ensalada de castañas y calabaza, y queso feta 675
- "Ravioli's" con apio y mantequilla de cacahuete en ensalada 775
- Empanadillas de setas y pato confitado 415
- Arcas de rana marinadas con salvia y gengibre 675
- Guiso de caracoles con tortilla japonesa 650
- Sushi de verduras con salvia japonesa 925
- MAKI de aguacate y pepino 750
- MAKI de gamba y lechón rebozado 1100
- Sushi variado 2500
- Huevos de codorniz escalfados con pisto y chistorra 450
- "Ravioli's botó" a la plancha 900
- Alcachofas guisadas con berengenas 625
- Tartar de avellana 675
- Salteado de arroz integral con shitake, espárragos y judías 625
- Bacalao con tomate y encurtidos 775
- "Civet de pato con manzana 875
- Mollejas de ternera, col lombarda y patata 850
- Hígado de pato con pera y pimienta sichuan 800
- Alitas de pollo tandoori 975
- Surtido de quesos 675

* A partir de 5 comensales sólo se sirve menú degustación. *

= Postres =

- Piña colada con chupa-chups 450
- Helado de caki, plumb-cake y toffe 675
- Manzana reineta con bizcocho de frutos secos y helado de chocolate 675
- Trufas de chocolate 375

Grilled salt cod with marinated garlic and pickles
Bacalao con boniato y encurtidos

for 6 tapas
750g (1lb 10oz) piece thick salt cod fillet,
taken from the middle of the cod
150g (5¹/₂oz) cloves garlic
olive oil
white wine vinegar
500g (1lb 2oz) sweet potatoes
black pepper
100g (3¹/₂oz) pickled gherkins, rinsed
of vinegar
200g (7oz) black olives
200g (3¹/₂oz) capers, rinsed of vinegar,
brine or salt
2 tbsp chopped flat-leaf parsley

Bacalao returns to conquer, but with a distinctive Catalan twist, as its velvety texture and gentle flavour sharply contrasts with the pickles. If you prefer a main course, double the quantity of sweet potato and serve the cod on a bed of mash.

1 Cut the salt cod into four equal pieces, cover with water and leave to de-salt for 48 hours, changing the water twice a day.

2 At the same time, marinate the garlic. Peel all the cloves and sauté them in a few tbsp olive oil until golden. Lift them out of the pan and put them in a jar. Add enough oil and vinegar (²/₃ oil to ¹/₃ vinegar) to cover.

3 Bake the sweet potatoes in their skins for 45 minutes to an hour at 180°C (350°F) Gas mark 4. They should be soft. Slit them open, remove the flesh and mash with a little olive oil and black pepper until very smooth.

4 Lift the salt cod out of the water and pat it dry. Brush each fillet with olive oil and set them on foil on a grill pan. Grill until golden on top, then turn the heat down and continue to grill until cooked through.

5 Transfer the cod to a platter and arrange the gherkins, black olives, capers and garlic cloves over and around it.

6 Sprinkle with the parsley and serve with the sweet potato mash.

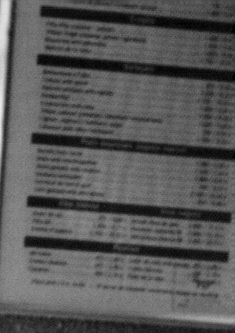

Josep Manubens   Cal Pep, Barcelona

The bottom line of Cal Pep is its unpretentiousness: good quality fresh fare is prepared quickly, cheerfully and in a straightforward way - a reflection of Pep (the nickname of Josep Manubens) himself. There is no fixed menu, as the tapas and raciones change according to what's in season, but the dishes on offer each day are expertly recited by the cheerful staff and the produce is cooked right in front of you. 'The fishermen only catch what's available, so I go along with that,' says Pep. 'I'll buy local seafood at the Lonja [Barcelona's wholesale fish market], go further afield along the Costa Brava for larger fish and buy Atlantic fish from the Boquería.'

Pep enjoys the company of his customers as much as he enjoys the freshness of the food. 'I never liked restaurants with tables, they're boring,' he says emphatically, 'so the obvious choice for me was to create a bar; that means there's constant contact. The food can be as good as it is in a five-star restaurant, but there's more charm and it's more fun for everyone.' Ever aware of practicalities, Pep realises that many of his customers need to eat in a hurry and, because of the style of the food and the bar, they can do exactly that. Now, 24 years after Cal Pep opened, it is an institution and Pep is revered among Barcelona's new generation of chefs.

Chilled potato, tomato and anchovy loaf
Pastel de anchoa

for 8 tapas

*500g (1lb 2oz) cooked potatoes,
mashed and pushed through a sieve
or potato ricer*

9 tbsp extra virgin olive oil

3 tbsp white wine vinegar

salt and pepper to taste

16 fresh anchovy fillets

*2-3 ripe tomatoes, peeled, seeded
and chopped*

*85g (3oz) black olives, pitted and
finely chopped*

This deliciously different recipe makes the most of some of Spain's staple ingredients - anchovies, tomatoes and potatoes. If you can't find fresh anchovies, choose some that have been marinated in vinegar, drain them and marinate them in olive oil for a few hours before using.

1 Put the mashed potatoes in a bowl. Prepare a vinaigrette with the oil, vinegar, salt and pepper and stir $^2/_3$ of it into the potatoes. Leave for at least 1 hour to let the flavours meld.

2 Place the anchovies in a shallow dish and dress them with the rest of the vinaigrette. Leave them to macerate for at least 1 hour. (If you are using ready-marinated anchovies, just drain them and carry on with the recipe.)

3 To form the loaf, cover the bottom of a 20 x 20cm (8 x 8-inch) tin with the anchovies. Spoon the chopped tomatoes over them, and spread a 1 cm ($^1/_2$-inch) thick layer of mashed potatoes over the tomatoes. Refrigerate for at least 1 hour.

4 To serve, unmould the loaf, anchovy-side-up, on to a platter, then sprinkle it with the black olives and cut it into slices.

Clams and ham in chilli sauce
Almejas con jamón

for 4 tapas

300g (10¹/₂oz) fresh clams, thoroughly cleaned (discard any that do not close)
60g (2¹/₄oz) ham, cut in thin strips
1 medium red chilli pepper, seeded and finely chopped
2 tbsp olive oil for sautéing
2 cloves garlic, minced
2 tbsp finely chopped flat-leaf parsley
2 tbsp white wine
salt and pepper to taste

The classic Catalan combination of sea and mountain ingredients features in this Cal Pep favourite. It is a simple but highly-flavoured dish that can easily be expanded to become a main course. Use mussels if you can't get hold of clams.

1 In a *paellera* or large frying pan, sauté the clams, ham and chilli pepper in hot oil until the clams begin to open.

2 Add the garlic, parsley, wine, salt and pepper, and continue to cook for about 2 more minutes. Discard any clams that have not opened. Spoon out into small bowls, pouring the sauce over last, and serve.

Tricky tortilla
Tortilla cachonda

for 4 tapas
olive oil for frying
100g (3¹/₂oz) chorizo or other spicy cured sausage, thinly sliced
2 medium potatoes, cooked, peeled and sliced
¹/₂ small onion, finely chopped and sautéed until soft
3 eggs, beaten
salt and pepper to taste
2 tbsp alioli

for the alioli
2 cloves garlic
sea salt
1 egg yolk
125ml (4fl oz) olive oil
lemon juice to taste
salt and white pepper to taste

You hardly know this is an omelette, albeit Spanish-style, when it appears on Pep's lengthy bar because it is covered in a deliciously thick layer of creamy *alioli* – hence the dish's name. Cut a slice, however, and you know you're in the realm of *tortilla*. If you have a small frying-pan, so much the better to make individual *tortillas*, but this dish also works as one large *tortilla*.

1 Make the alioli by crushing the garlic with a little sea salt. Stir the egg yolk into this and beat. Add the olive oil a drop at a time, continuing to beat and increasing the stream of oil as more becomes incorporated. You should end up with a thick, creamy mixture. When you've added all the oil, add the lemon juice, salt and pepper to taste. Cover and refrigerate immediately.

2 To make the *tortilla*, heat 1 tbsp olive oil in a small frying pan and sauté the chorizo quickly until just browned. Add the potatoes and onion and stir to brown.

3 In a bowl, mix the chorizo, potatoes and onion with the eggs. Put 2 tbsp oil into the pan and pour the mixture back into it. Cook over a low heat for 3 minutes. When the omelette is firm but not dry, cover the frying pan with a flat plate and flip to turn the omelette out on to the plate. Slide the omelette back into the pan and cook for 3 minutes, to brown the other side. Cool for 5 minutes, then serve with a layer of alioli.

Curly white endive in garlic oil
Escarola al ajillo

for 6 tapas
1 curly endive (frisée) lettuce, washed, coarse leaves removed
3 cloves garlic, thinly sliced
6 tbsp olive oil
salt and pepper to taste
2 tbsp white wine vinegar
250g (9oz) assorted cold cured sausages, thinly sliced

Pep's salad tapa is a delicious blend of hot, garlicky dressing with crunchy lettuce and meaty sausage slices. In Catalonia, *embutidos* (cured sausages) vary considerably in shape, size, texture and flavour, so try as many examples as you can – from salami to chorizo.

1 Pull the endive apart and put the leaves in a bowl or on a serving platter.

2 Quickly sauté the garlic in very hot olive oil until golden brown. Season with salt and pepper, remove from the heat and add the vinegar.

3 Just before serving, pour the hot garlic dressing over the endive and toss it together with the sausage slices.

RIOJA and OLD CASTILE

José María
José María

Carlos Martínez
Meay Espinosa
Casa Pali

Miguel Reguera García
Momo

*T*ake a wrong turning in Old Castile and you might find yourself twisting endlessly through the sierra, leaving wheatfields behind to be replaced by rolling hills studded with flocks of sheep, then by stark outcrops overlooking an apparently bleak wasteland. In a swathe of high plateau (the ubiquitous *meseta*), this vast region of Spain extends northwards from Madrid before hitting the natural mountain barrier of the Sierra Cantábrica. The name 'castillo' itself, meaning 'castle', harks back to the 9th century, when the region – or more precisely the Ebro and Duero rivers that slice through it – was the

menus written in stylised gothic script, storks' nests atop church towers, weathered faces, meat... and more meat, including a breed of cow thought to be the oldest in Europe (the Negra Ibérica of Ávila). This is the land that produced Isabela la Católica, the infamous or astute (depending on one's historical viewpoint) unifier of Spain and conqueror of the Moors in 1492. Long before her birth, pilgrims had left their symbolic mark as they traipsed through northern Castile along the Way of St James in the scorching sun or bone-chilling wind. Centuries later, Catholicism and conservatism still run

'Here the heart of medieval Spain, flickering with the ghosts of pilgrims and hidalgos, is characterised by gloomy bars of dark varnished wood, menus written in stylised gothic script, storks' nests atop church towers, weathered faces, meat... and more meat'

frontline in the long conflict between Moors and Christians. Crenellated castles proliferated on every hilltop, and were often built over Celtiberian and/or Roman predecessors.

But this is the 21st century and, although the castle silhouettes still loom evocatively, life has moved on in the villages and towns below. Yet Old Castile (as opposed to New Castile south of Madrid) still symbolises a quintessential Spain; not the exuberant flamenco style of the south, but one of austerity, silent cloisters, grains, pulses, organic meat and velvety, full-bodied wine. Here the heart of medieval Spain, flickering with the ghosts of pilgrims and *hidalgos*, is characterised by gloomy bars of dark varnished wood,

deep, producing a firmly-entrenched respect for earthy foods and time-honoured methods.

Biting into the northern perimeter of this region, Rioja shares some Castilian attributes, but its personality and land are visibly richer, more fertile, more generous and more open. The name 'Rioja' itself is synonymous with Spain's best-known wine: vineyards stripe the undulating hills that descend to the Río Ebro, and *bodegas* (wineries) cluster around the wine-capitals of Logroño and Haro. In September, the wine-festival is celebrated so single-mindedly that, for several nights, Logroño's streets are jammed with carousers until dawn, all exuding a *joie de vivre* that may well be massaged by the vintage Rioja that is coursing through their veins.

Wine aside, Rioja plays a major role as northern Spain's market garden, producing red peppers, artichokes, asparagus, aubergines and countless other shiny vegetables that tumble colourfully on to market stalls. Lamb is a culinary mainstay, while higher up in the forested sierra, partridge, quail, rabbit and deer take over: ingredients for the robust fare that compensates for the region's freezing cold winters.

Old Castile shares this taste, alongside a love of meat. Chefs wax lyrical on the sensual delight of a recipe using the neck glands of lamb or, that other popular tender morsel, the pig's ear. Absolutely nothing from the pig is wasted: even the hair becomes bristle for tooth- or nail-brushes. Suckling pigs are a delicacy of Segovia, their little snouts poking over many a restaurant or butcher's counter, and they are now down to acquire DOC (*Denominación de Origen Controllado*) status. Cows are popular, with *cecina* (cured beef) a much sought-after product of León. The tradition of cured meat started with the Romans (*cecina* derives from the Latin *siccina*) and for centuries it consisted of horsemeat, the perfect chewy, long-lasting warrior food. Times and tastes changed, and beef took over, although *cecina de caballo* can still be found in remote Castilian villages.

Meanwhile, the pig continues on its path: Salamanca is renowned for its velvety *jamón de guijuelo,* while pigs' ears, cheeks, tripe, liver and trotters shape elaborate recipes, and the blood becomes *morcilla,* a black pudding variously combining rice, onion, cumin and pine nuts. Nearly every tapas bar will serve this – hot, juicy and spicy – with a neighbouring plate of cold chorizo, the spicy pork sausage coloured and flavoured with Murcian or Extremaduran paprika.

In the realm of pulses and grains, Old Castile is the master. Sacks of them fill specialist shops and market stalls, and menus feature many incarnations, all dependent on the original quality product: lentils from La Armunya; white kidney beans from El Barco de Ávila; white, black or streaked *judiones* (big beans) from La Granja; chickpeas from Zamora. Wheat being an agricultural mainstay of the plains, bread appears in countless forms. Hardly surprising then, that José María's highly-rated restaurant in Segovia has an altar niche devoted to '*pan y vin*' (bread and wine). Then there are pine nuts and chicory from Valladolid, truffles from Soría, asparagus from Tudela and goat's and sheep's cheese from all over. And in the towering moutains of Picos de Europa, which divide Old Castile from the green pastures of Cantabria, blue cheese is produced. The list is endless, and so is the potential to make tapas. But innovation is slow to permeate this conservative region, and it is no surprise that the one chef to successfully indulge in *la nueva cocina* is a Riojan (although not a tapas chef), Francis Paniego, who reigns at Echaurren, high in the Sierra de la Demanda.

The secret to this region is to get lost. Stock up on some wine straight from a *bodega*, pack a basket with market goodies and head for the hills. Then, as night falls, make for any of the large towns and join the throng at the tapas bars. Later, back at home, the closest you can come to this spirit is to grab some red peppers and an aubergine and recreate some of the offerings. Then uncork that bottle of vintage Rioja. You won't regret it.

José María   José María, Segovia

You can't avoid the suckling pigs at José María: this is Segovia's temple to the cochinillo's delights, where some 8,000 suckling pigs are dished up annually. There's even a bronze effigy of one snuggling contentedly outside. José María himself exudes energy, warmth and enthusiasm, despite running a team of 50 staff and catering for hundreds of faithful customers every weekend. He has even cooked for King Juan Carlos.

José María is from a farming family, based just outside Segovia, and he had a love of quality Castilian foods instilled in him as a child. The secret of his success is his fidelity to local ingredients, which he juggles within a traditional framework, making slight 'modernist' adjustments. 'The main protagonist of each of my dishes is the central food – everything else is delicately complementary. Castile is a self-assured region, but it lacks fantasy, so I'm careful,' he says. Despite this caution, the tapas served in José María's heaving front bar are delicious and he constantly reinvents his menu (apart, that is, from the suckling pig!). 'We try lots of things to make interesting new dishes, but many aren't viable for making on a large scale in the restaurant,' he bemoans. When he opened this bar-restaurant in 1982, he declared 'I have a face and two hands, so why not use them?' The diners' response? Absolutely!

Marinated lamb and watercress salad
Ensalada de corderito lechal escabechado con manzana confitada

for 6 tapas
1 x 1.8kg (4lb) leg of spring lamb, bone removed (boned weight)
salt and pepper to taste
flour for coating
1 litre (1³/4 pints) virgin olive oil
375ml (13fl oz) red wine vinegar
100g (3¹/2oz) mushrooms, sliced
6 cloves garlic, crushed
3 leeks, chopped
100g (3¹/2oz) carrots, sliced
1 sprig thyme
3 bay leaves
1 large tart apple, peeled, cored and cut into fine slices lengthways
1 bunch watercress, washed and stems removed
1 carrot, cut into julienne strips
leaves from 2 endives, cut into strips
4 baby tomatoes, halved

for the vinaigrette
1 tbsp red wine vinegar
3¹/2 tbsp extra virgin olive oil

Marinades are a Castilian tradition, used for conserving fish and lean meat. The lamb preparation in this recipe is time-consuming and a little complex, but the end easily justifies the means as the marinade perfectly complements the lamb.

1 Around 4 days before serving, season the leg of lamb with salt and pepper, dip it in flour and brown it in a little olive oil. Place the meat in a casserole and add the olive oil, vinegar, mushrooms, garlic, leeks, carrots, thyme, bay leaves, and more salt and pepper to taste. Cover the pan, bring to the boil and simmer gently for 1 hour 15 minutes.

2 Remove from the heat, cool, and then refrigerate for 3 days in the casserole in which the dish was cooked. On the third day, transfer the contents to a different container, add the apple slices and refrigerate for 1 more day.

3 To prepare the salad, remove the meat from the marinade and slice it thinly. Remove the apple slices and mash them with a fork. Remove the mushrooms and set them aside.

4 Strain the marinade and make a vinaigrette using 175ml (6fl oz) of the strained liquid. Add the vinegar and extra virgin olive oil and season.

5 Just before serving, arrange the watercress on a plate and drizzle with vinaigrette. On top of the watercress put a layer of the lamb, then carrots, then endives and then mushrooms and tomatoes, and top with the apple confit. Drizzle on the vinaigrette and serve.

Marinated lamb and watercress salad (left)
Leeks with a summer vegetable vinaigrette
(page 75)

Sautéed pork liver with mushrooms and pine nuts
Salteado de hígado de cochinillo con setas y piñones

for 6 tapas

3 young pigs' livers, coarsely chopped
olive oil
50g (1³/₄oz) wild mushrooms, sliced
1 clove garlic, minced
1 tbsp white wine vinegar
15g (¹/₂oz) pine nuts

José María prepares this dish with liver from a recently slaughtered suckling pig. However, the strong flavour means that the other ingredients can easily be overlooked by diners so, if possible, use mushrooms to balance the flavours.

1 Sauté the pork liver in a little olive oil and set aside. Sauté the mushrooms and garlic in 2 tbsp olive oil until tender. Add the liver and heat through.

2 Create a mound of the liver and mushrooms on a serving plate, splash with the vinegar, garnish with the pine nuts and serve immediately.

'The main protagonist of each of my dishes is the central food – everything else is delicately complementary. Castile is a serious, self-assured region, but it lacks fantasy, so I'm careful.'

Millennium salad
Ensalada del milenio

for 8 tapas

1 large avocado, halved, stoned
and peeled
olive oil
60g (2¹/₄oz) fresh goat's or cream cheese, beaten until smooth
1 red pepper, roasted, peeled and cut into strips
1 bunch watercress
4 anchovy fillets, drained of oil
1 tbsp finely snipped chives

for the vinaigrette

1¹/₂ tbsp white wine vinegar
4 tbsp extra virgin olive oil
salt and pepper to taste

José María's most recent invention, created for the new millennium, is a winning combination of flavours and textures. The presentation of this tapa is paramount, as it hinges on the layering of the ingredients into a tower of textures and colours.

1 At least 1 day before serving, place the avocado in a small saucepan, cover with olive oil and cook over a very low heat, without boiling, for 30 minutes. Remove from the heat and steep in the oil overnight if possible.

2 Shortly before serving, lift the avocado halves out of the oil and spread a thin layer of cheese over each one. Lay the strips of pepper on top.

3 Make a vinaigrette by mixing the vinegar and olive oil and then seasoning. Form a nest with the watercress, dress with a little vinaigrette and lay the anchovy fillets on top in a diamond shape. Place the avocado halves in the nest, garnish with chives and drizzle with the rest of the vinaigrette.

4 Cut each halved avocado into quarters and serve immediately.

Leeks with a summer vegetable vinaigrette
Puerros del monasterio con vinagreta

for 6 tapas

*12 slim leeks, white portion only,
stripped of outer layer and root*

salt to taste

1 tbsp olive oil

1 onion, finely chopped

1 small red pepper, finely chopped

1 small green pepper, finely chopped

*100g (3¹/₂oz) gherkins, rinsed of
vinegar and finely chopped*

*100g (3¹/₂oz) capers, rinsed of vinegar,
brine or salt and finely chopped*

2 small green tomatoes, finely chopped

125ml (4fl oz) extra virgin olive oil

2 tbsp white wine vinegar

1 bunch watercress

For centuries, leeks were relegated to support roles in Castilian cooking, but they are back on centre stage, particularly in the province of Segovia, where they are extensively cultivated. In this recipe, the colourful vegetable vinaigrette that covers the stacked white leeks makes for a particularly refreshing summer tapa.

1 At least 1 hour before serving, cook the leeks in plenty of salted boiling water and 1 tbsp olive oil for about 12 minutes. Drain, cool the leeks and cut them in half lengthways.

2 Prepare the vegetable vinaigrette by mixing together the onion, peppers, gherkins, capers and tomatoes. Coat with the olive oil and wine vinegar. Season with salt to taste.

3 Just before serving, stack the leeks on a plate on a bed of watercress, and cover with the chopped vegetables.

Traditional Segovian pork and potato 'fry-up'
Tentempié tradicional segoviano con patatas nuevas

for 6 tapas

*500g (1lb 2oz) new potatoes, peeled
and thinly sliced*

1 large onion, thinly sliced

olive oil for frying

4 eggs

*1 x 100g (3¹/₂oz) piece of roast pork,
cut into strips about 1cm (¹/₂-inch) wide*

salt and pepper to taste

4 slices of fried French bread

This hearty Segovian dish has strong rural and wintry overtones straight from the heart of Old Castile. It traditionally filled empty peasant stomachs with an artful combination of left-over pork and seasonal new potatoes. Quick to prepare, it is more than just a substantial tapa, as it works equally well for brunch or as an evening snack.

1 Fry the potatoes and onion in plenty of olive oil over a low heat for about 20 minutes. They should be just tender. Drain the excess oil from the frying pan and continue to brown the vegetables lightly.

2 Break the eggs directly over the potatoes and onions. Add the pork, season well, and stir to mix all the ingredients together. Cook until the eggs are just set. Serve immediately, accompanied by the fried bread.

Carlos Martínez, Meay Espinosa   Casa Pali, Logroño

Halfway along Calle Laurel, Logroño's legendary haunt of tapas bars, you will spot a deep, narrow bar, usually bursting with tapa-hoppers who are addicted to the house speciality of fried aubergine. During early afternoons and throughout the evenings, this narrow pedestrian street throngs with people of all ages, styles and social origins; in all of Spain, it is hard to find a crowd more dedicated to the movable feast. As their hunting-ground encompasses an easy stroll of about 200 metres, competition is hot and the chefs are kept on their toes.

Casa Pali opened in 1994, when Carlos Martínez and his partner Meay Espinosa decided there weren't enough vegetable-based tapas in Logroño. 'We decided to make something healthier than the tapas other bars were making, and the aubergine became our symbol,' recounts Carlos. In works of art, created by friends, on the walls of Casa Pali, Rioja's plumpest, shiniest vegetable is recreated in styles from Pop Art to classical still life. 'We're not trying to do anything sophisticated, but it's different from the usual tapas fare,' says Carlos. Try these dishes and you'll know why the bar's a success.

Fried asparagus, ham and cheese bundles
Espárragos con jamón de York y queso

for 4 tapas
*4 thin slices mild, easy to melt cheese,
such as French Port Salut
4 asparagus spears, cooked until
just tender
4 thin slices cooked ham
beaten egg for coating
flour for coating
olive oil for frying*

The classic marriage of ham and cheese is made more interesting by the texture and subtle flavour of the asparagus. Riojans love tinned asparagus spears so, for authenticity's sake, you needn't worry about finding the fresh variety – but use it if you prefer the extra crunch. This is one of Logroño's rare tapas that needs a knife and fork.

1 Place 1 slice of the mild cheese and 1 asparagus spear on each slice of cooked ham and carefully roll each one up to form a cylinder.

2 Dip the ham rolls in the egg and then the flour, then fry them in a little hot oil until they are golden brown. Serve immediately.

beicon,
queso, setas

pechuga, lechuga,
queso azul

paté con queso

Fried aubergine with cheese
Berenjena con queso

for 4 tapas

4 thin slices of tangy, easy-to-melt cheese, such as French Chaumes, cut to fit the aubergine
8 thin slices of aubergine
salt to taste
2 beaten eggs for coating
flour for coating
olive oil for frying

This, Casa Pali's flagship tapa, is easy and quick to prepare. It can even be half-cooked in advance and re-fried at the last minute. Your guests will need small knives and forks to devour it.

1 For each tapa, place 1 slice of cheese between 2 slices of aubergine.

2 Season each sandwich of aubergine with salt, then dip it in egg and then flour. Fry in a little olive oil over a medium heat until golden on both sides. Serve hot.

Ham croquettes
Croquetas de jamón

for 6 tapas
50g (1³/₄oz) butter
175g (6oz) flour
400ml (14fl oz) milk
1 small onion, finely chopped
1 tbsp olive oil
50g (1³/₄oz) Serrano ham,
finely chopped
salt and pepper
2 beaten eggs for coating
fine, dry breadcrumbs for coating
100ml (3¹/₂fl oz) olive oil for frying

Competition in the ham croquettes stakes is ruthless. All over Spain, some sad attempts and a few delectable ones are created. The Casa Pali version is a rare bird, as it achieves the perfect blend of reassuring creaminess and smoky ham flavour in a deliciously crisp outer coating.

1 Melt the butter in a frying pan. Add the flour and stir for 3-4 minutes, until well blended, to form a roux. Take the pan off the heat and add the milk slowly, incorporating each addition into the roux and mixing until it is smooth before adding any more. Put the pan back on the heat and bring the milk up to the boil, stirring continually. The mixture should become very thick. Turn the heat down low and cook for about 5 minutes, stirring from time to time.

2 Gently sauté the onion in the olive oil until it is soft but not coloured. Add the pieces of ham.

3 Stir the onion and ham into the white sauce and season well with salt and pepper. Spread the mixture in a lightly greased pan to about 2cm (1 inch) thickness. Put in the fridge and chill for at least 2 hours.

4 When cool, cut the chilled mixture into small bars, then use your hands to shape each bar into a little cylinder.

5 Coat each croquette with egg and breadcrumbs. Pour about 8cm (3 inches) of olive oil into a pan and heat. Fry the croquettes a few at a time, until they are dark gold on the outside and warm and cooked in the middle. It's a good idea to test one to check whether your oil is at the optimum temperature; you don't want to brown the outside too much without also penetrating through to the middle of the croquette.

6 Drain on kitchen paper and either serve hot or at room temperature.

'We decided to make something healthier than the tapas other bars were making, and the aubergine became our symbol.'

Miguel Reguera García Momo, Salamanca

Opened in early 2001, Momo hums with life, bottles of more than 150 wines and an extensive menu of hot and cold tapas and raciones. With high-tech ventilation pipes beside chandeliers, 1950s red diner chairs and a steel-clad bar, Momo stands out for its design as well as for its Basque-style pintxos with a Castilian accent. 'I saw what tapas bars were doing in San Sebastián and Valladolid and decided to do something different for Salamanca,' says Miguel Reguera García, so he joined two partners to create Momo. Miguel is frank about having simply adapted some established recipes, but his strength lies in his taste for the best. 'I like everything on my menu, but there are things we don't do, such as Tortilla de patatas - you need one person dedicated to making it,' he says. Instead, Momo's menu features an abundance of cured meats, goat's and sheep's cheeses, leeks, peppers, courgettes and aubergines. From these, Miguel has created designer pintxos that are dressed to kill - minimally, of course.

Red pepper, leek, anchovy and cream cheese tarts
Queso, anchoa, pimiento y puerro sobre hojaldre

for 4 tapas

1 leek, white portion only
4 anchovy fillets, drained of oil
½ small red pepper, roasted, peeled and cut into 4 equal strips
4 x 10cm (4-inch) squares of puff pastry, cooked
100g (3½oz) cream cheese

This two-bite size tapa is quick to make as well as to consume, yet the pastry case makes it satisfyingly filling. The quantity of anchovy or red pepper can be increased according to your taste.

1 Cut the leek in half lengthways and cook it in boiling water until just tender. Drain and cut each half in half again lengthways.

2 Place 1 anchovy and 1 small strip of red pepper on each puff pastry square, then spread carefully with a quarter of the cream cheese. Top with a piece of the white leek.

3 Place under a grill for just long enough to heat through (about 3-4 minutes) and serve immediately.

Red pepper, leek, anchovy and cream cheese tarts

Ham, broad bean and alioli toasts (page 88)

Foie gras, courgette and bitter orange toasts (over)

Cream cheese and leek toasts
Puerros con crema de queso

for 4 tapas

75g (2³/₄oz) cream cheese
4 tbsp sunflower oil
20ml (³/₄fl oz) milk
2 slices white bread, crusts removed and cut in half
4 very fine leeks, cut in half lengthways, cooked and cooled
8 capers

The traditional Castilian leek is dominant in this tapa, and perfectly complemented by the cream cheese.

1 Mix the cheese, oil and milk in a blender until creamy.

2 Toast the bread and place 2 leek halves on each piece.

3 Cover with the cheese sauce and garnish with a caper at each end.

4 Place under the grill for 1 minute. Serve hot.

'I saw what tapas bars were doing in San Sebastián and Valladolid and decided to do something different for Salamanca.'

Foie gras, courgette and bitter orange toasts
Calabacín con foie gras

for 4 tapas

20g (³/₄oz) foie gras
8 x 3mm (¹/₈-inch) courgette slices
olive oil
4 slices French bread, cut on the diagonal
1 tbsp best bitter orange marmalade
black pepper to taste

This is an unusual combination of flavours, yet the end result is a wonderfully rich and luxurious tapa. Miguel uses foie mi-cuit, a superior version of foie gras with a more subtle flavour, but if you can't get hold of it, use foie gras.

1 For each tapa, sandwich a quarter of the foie gras between 2 courgette slices. Brush with a little oil and grill for 3 minutes on each side.

2 Toast the bread, spread a little marmalade on each slice, and top with a courgette and foie gras sandwich. Dust with pepper and serve at once.

GAMBAS
· SOLOMILLO
· ATÚN
· ANCHOA
· BOLETUS CON JAMÓN
· QUESO DE CABRA
· PIQUILLO CON GAMBAS
· PIQUILLO CON SOLOMILLO

· MEDALLÓN DE SOLOMILLO
· CALABACÍN CON FOIE
· LACÓN, ALCACHOFAS Y HABITAS
· JAMÓN IBERICO, HABITAS Y SALMÓN
· CECINA DE MORUCHA

Ham, artichoke, broad bean and alioli toasts
Jamón, alcachofa y habitas con ali oli

for 4 tapas

*4 slices French bread, cut on
the diagonal*
100g (3¹/₂oz) Serrano ham
12 broad beans, cooked and drained
*1 artichoke heart, cooked, drained, and
sliced in 4*
125g (4oz) Momo's alioli (recipe below)
paprika

This tapa and the following can be made together, offering alternative flavours but sharing the *alioli* topping. They are both simple to prepare, and the visual disguise of *alioli* leaves the ingredients as a surprise.

1 Toast the bread and on each slice place a quarter of the ham, folded to fit the bread, 3 broad beans and a slice of artichoke heart.

2 Cover each tapa with a generous amount of *alioli* and dust with paprika before placing under a very hot grill for 15-20 seconds.

Ham, broad bean, smoked salmon and alioli toasts
Jamón, salmón, habitas con alioli y queso

for 4 tapas

4 slices white bread
1 slice cooked ham
12 broad beans, cooked and drained
*125ml (4fl oz) Momo's alioli
(recipe below)*
1 slice of smoked salmon, chopped

Smoked salmon is a favourite tapa ingredient – be sure to use the best you can find for this simple tapa.

1 Toast the bread and on each slice place a quarter of the ham, folded to fit the bread, and 3 broad beans.

2 Cover each tapa with a generous amount of alioli, then garnish with a little smoked salmon at each end before placing under a hot grill for 15-20 seconds.

Momo's alioli
Momo's alioli

for 4 tapas

75g (2³/₄oz) cream cheese
2 cloves garlic
4 tbsp sunflower oil
20ml (³/₄fl oz) milk

Alioli should be as fresh as possible, so you should make it as close to the preparation of the tapas as you can.

1 Mix all the ingredients in a blender until creamy.

MADRID

José Angel Valladeres
Paloma Tatay
Andrés Goméz
Fernando Estrada
Albur

Luis Benavente
Bocaito

Joaquín Campos
Casa Matute

José Luis Ruiz Solaguren
José Luis

Madrid may be Spain's political capital, but it is also one of the country's youngest cities in every sense of the word. Only developed as the capital in the 1560s by the new Hapsburg kings, it cannot boast the same historical sweep as Spain's other great cities. Nor can it claim much of a truly indigenous cuisine. Yet into this growing metropolis has come a cosmopolitan mix of immigrants hailing from every far-flung corner of the peninsula, and the population has tripled since the 1950s.

Food being a national obsession, these new citizens have brought with them their native regions – from Galicia

It was in the dry electric air of the capital, too, that the cathartic 1980s *movida madrileña*, the revitalising 'Madrid movement' of post-Franco Spain, was spearheaded, bringing with it a sea change in political outlook, cultural direction and freedom, and social mores. The *madrileños* turned up the gas in their ovens and restocked their fridges, embracing everything they had been deprived of during the long decades of repression. Avocados, broccoli, raspberries – such foods were all unknown before the late 1970s. Food diversity became an integral part of the hot revolutionary package of sex, drugs

'Go to any grocery store and you will find produce from every corner of the peninsula. Fleshy octopus from windswept Galicia spread their tentacles over market stalls and shiny Valencian oranges are juiced to frothy perfection at breakfast cafés.'

to Andalucia to Extremadura – in the form of a plethora of specialist restaurants and tapas bars. And into their kitchens has gone produce from the city's shops and markets, where a mouth-watering array of shapes, textures and colours can be found. Over the last 15 years or so, vast improvements in Spain's infrastructure have clarified Madrid's position as the gastronomic heart of the nation. All roads may lead to Rome, but all Spanish roads – laden with lorry-loads of food – lead to Madrid. As a result, whatever their origin, most trainee chefs worth their salt pass through the kitchens of the capital's restaurants before, more often than not, returning to their beloved home towns.

and rock 'n' roll, in the atmosphere epitomised by Pedro Almodóvar's frenetic films and a string of night-clubs and tapas bars open until dawn. Like New York and New Orleans before it, Madrid became a 'city that never sleeps'.

Go to any local grocery store and you will find a mind-boggling array of fresh, vacuum-packed, bottled and canned produce from every corner of the peninsula. Fleshy octopuses from windswept Galicia spread their tentacles over market stalls or stew in cavernous cooking pots; fine slivers of *mojama* (cured tuna) from Cádiz accompany a glass of *fino*; Andalucian olives glisten on every bar-top, and shiny Valencian oranges are juiced to frothy perfection at breakfast cafés. The one misnomer is the chicken's egg: that *tortilla* awaiting punters on the bar counter is not always whisked up from fresh eggs but, instead, concocted from powdered extract. While it may be disappointing for purists, this recent enforcement of health regulations prevents outbreaks of salmonella in the sizzling summers.

Then there are *jamón* and *bacalao*, preserved by the same methods for centuries. Armies of legs of *jamón serrano* (literally 'sawn ham', but cured like all *jamón* and usually made from white-footed pigs), its superior cousin *jamón ibérico* (from black-coated pigs), also known as *jamón de pata negra* ('ham of the black foot'), are displayed behind the bars of central Madrid. The city even boasts a chain of 'ham museums', and *jamón's* immortalised 18th century image, signed by the artist Luis Eugenio Meléndez, hangs in the hallowed halls of the Prado. Times may change, but the presentation of *jamón* does not. Pretension and artifice are unheard of: no designer packaging is needed as the truth lies firmly in the taste. Such is *jamón's* primordial role in the *madrileños'* diet, you can imagine duels fought over the relative merits of different hams, between the august facades of the Plaza Mayor.

Sharing equal status with *jamón* is *bacalao*, or salt cod, whose capture has inspired many a fanatical confrontation between Galician, Cantabrian or Basque fishermen and their counterparts from Cornwall or Brittany. First landed on the peninsula 500 years ago from the boats of Basque fishermen, this much-prized staple conquered the country, Madrid included. You may find its flaky white flesh fried in batter to make dreamlike puffs (*Soldaditos*), in smoked *bacalao* pâté or as creamy croquettes. In central Madrid, at 1.30pm on any weekday, a motley crowd of besuited businessmen, diminutive grannies, workmen and lithe young teenagers jostles in hungry harmony inside Casa Labra, a bar of elegantly faded splendour. The reason? This is the last source of Madrid's traditional freshly fried *Soldaditos* (whimsically named 'Little soldiers from Pavia') as well as croquettes filled with a cream of the deified food. The rhythm is regular as bags are filled with *Soldaditos* to take away, drinks are poured and mouths opened and closed over the golden morsels. Then history creeps in when you learn that a decade after its founding in 1869, this bar witnessed the inception of the Spanish Socialist Party.

If there is one dish that Madrid can hoist as its culinary flag, it is the *Cocido*. This slow-cooked casserole of meat, sausage, chickpeas and vegetables, its components eaten separately over several courses, reflects the need for sustenance during the capital's bitter winters. On the other hand, you may spot a slim young thing devouring an entire *Cocido* in mid-summer, such is the *madrileños'* enthusiasm for this dish. A tapa that has emerged from it is the *Caldo*, a cup of hot meat broth often consumed before embarking on alcohol and more substantial snacks. In this case, head for the illustrious Lhardy, which has been serving Madrid's quintessential version out of an ornate silver samovar since 1839. Tripe is another Madrid favourite, producing, for example, *Callos a la madrileña*, a tripe casserole kick-started with chorizo and chillies, that is consumed in small portions in many a tapas bar.

The tapas in Madrid seem endless, providing a synopsis of everything Spain produces. Repeat them in your own kitchen – with or without that rapier.

José Angel Valladeres
Paloma Tatay
Andrés Goméz
Fernando Estrada Albur, Madrid

Young and wild at heart, the four people behind Albur share a passion for Spain's regional specialities. Being located in the Malaseña district has helped Albur become a social crossroads for young professionals, politicos and craftspeople, all of whom mix around the long bar or tables at the back. From 2.30pm onwards, it's hard to squeeze in, as the changing menu is a magnet for locals, and vast portions of regional Spanish food are consumed.

Mini, the nickname of José Angel Valladeres, is the spokesman. This ebullient man, from a remote (albeit foodie) valley of Old Castile, set up Albur with Paloma Tatay, Andrés Goméz and Fernando Estrada, the only protagonist to have run a restaurant. From this team emerged a tapas menu that shifts from morcilla (black pudding) and 14-month-old cecina (cured beef) from León to cheese from La Serena in Extremadura and snails from Gerona.

'We go out and look for the best products, then order them directly from the producers, so it's much cheaper,' recounts Mini. 'When we opened in 1995, most of Madrid's tapas bars served Manchego food, so we decided to bring the best of the regions here,' he continues. 'In Castilian "albur" means "making a bet" and, by extension, taking risks or being lucky. In Mexican Spanish, "albur" came to mean "a play on words",' explains Mini. 'So the word travelled with our ancestors, then came back transformed. That's what we are doing with food - looking for new directions based on what exists and risking innovation. So far we've been lucky.' With imminent expansion into adjoining premises, Albur's star is still on the rise.

Mushrooms in parsley sauce
Champiñónes en salsa verde

for 8 tapas
100ml (3¹/₂fl oz) virgin olive oil
6 cloves garlic, minced
¹/₂ red chilli pepper or 2 dried
cayenne peppers
1kg (2¹/₄lb) fresh, white mushrooms,
cleaned and halved or quartered,
depending on their size
salt and pepper to taste
1 tbsp flour

for the sauce
2 cloves garlic, minced
leaves from a small bunch of flat-leaf
parsley, finely chopped
100ml (3¹/₂fl oz) white wine
salt and pepper to taste

Albur serves this tapa in a shallow terracotta dish – perfect for the juicy mushrooms and their green sauce. This dish is quite delicious and the ingredients are available all year round.

1 Mix the garlic, parsley, white wine, salt and pepper for the sauce in a small bowl and set aside.

2 Pour the olive oil into a casserole, add the garlic and cook gently until tender. Add the chilli pepper and mushrooms and increase the heat. Cook, stirring constantly, until the juice has been drawn out of the mushrooms. Season and continue to simmer over a moderately high heat for about 10 minutes, stirring occasionally, until the juice has evaporated.

3 Sprinkle the flour over the mushrooms and stir to blend well. Remove the pan from the heat and slowly add the sauce ingredients, making sure you incorporate them well. Return the pan to the heat and bring to the boil, stirring all the time. Simmer for 5 minutes, until you have a fairly thick sauce; add a little water if you want to thin it down. Serve hot.

Mussels in spicy sauce
Mejillones en salsa picante

for 4 tapas
4 bay leaves
salt and pepper to taste
1kg (2¹/₄lb) mussels, scrubbed and
any that do not close discarded
50ml (2fl oz) olive oil
1 large onion, chopped
6 cloves garlic, minced
¹/₂ red chilli pepper, seeded and
finely chopped
1 tsp flour
1¹/₂ tsp hot smoked Spanish paprika
(pimentón de la Vera)
100g (3¹/₂oz) Cebreiro cheese, or similar
sharp cheese that melts well, grated

It is essential to leave the grilling of this recipe until just before you serve it – that way it tastes fresh and hot. Find mussels that are as plump, juicy and fresh as possible and choose cheese such as a mature Cheddar, with a sharp, tangy flavour.

1 In a deep, heavy pan, bring about 100ml (3¹/₂fl oz) water, with 2 bay leaves and a pinch of salt, to the boil. Add the mussels, cover the pan and cook for about 4-5 minutes, until the shells open.

2 Remove the mussels from the pan, discard any that haven't opened, then remove the lids from the rest and throw the empty shells away. Place the mussels in their half-shells in a shallow oven-proof dish, pour the cooking liquid over them and set them aside.

3 Heat the oil in a large frying pan. Add the onion, garlic, chilli and the other 2 bay leaves. Sauté gently over a low heat until the onion turns golden.

4 Stir in the flour and paprika and cook for 1 minute, stirring constantly.

5 Take the pan off the heat and slowly add the mussel cooking liquid, stirring all the time to incorporate it well. Put the pan back on the heat and cook until the sauce thickens. Remove from the heat and mix in a blender to achieve a smooth sauce.

6 Return the sauce to the pan, add the mussels and cook for 3-4 minutes to warm through. Arrange the mussels and sauce in a serving bowl, sprinkle with grated cheese, and put under a medium grill until the cheese has melted. Serve immediately.

Red peppers stuffed with black pudding
Pimientos rellenos de morcilla

for 8 tapas
8 small red peppers (preferably piquillocan be canned) or 4 regular red peppers

olive oil

200g (7oz) black pudding (preferably from León)

1 egg, beaten

2 leaves fresh basil, finely chopped

25g (1oz) butter

2 tbsp flour

150ml (1/4 pint) milk

75g (2³/4oz) chickpeas, cooked and drained

1/2 tsp ground ginger

salt and pepper to taste

15g (1/2oz) pine nuts

Spain offers endless varieties of black pudding, but other countries are less inventive, so find the best you can. The combination of the dark blood sausage and the fresh red pepper is quintessentially Spanish, and Albur has raised this classic dish to new heights by adding basil, ginger and pine nuts.

1 If you are using canned *piquillo* peppers, just drain and halve them. If you are using raw peppers, brush them with olive oil and grill them until tender and partly black and blistered. Leave them aside until cool enough to handle, then peel off the skins, halve and seed them and set aside.

2 Fry the black pudding in an ungreased frying pan, breaking it into small pieces with a wooden spoon as you cook it. Remove from the heat, add the egg and stir until the egg has set. Add the basil and stir. Set aside.

3 Melt the butter, add the flour and stir to form a roux. Cook for 2 minutes. Remove from the heat and slowly add the milk, beating wel;. Bring back to the boil, stirring, until the sauce has thickened. Purée the chickpeas and add to the sauce. Add the ginger and seasoning. Simmer for 4 minutes. Pour into a shallow oven-proof dish.

4 Fill the pepper halves with the black pudding mixture, arrange them on the chickpea sauce and sprinkle with pine nuts. Cook at 180°C (350°F) Gas mark 4 for 10 minutes and serve.

Lamb stew
Caldereta de cordero

for 6 tapas
2 tbsp olive oil

700g (1lb 9oz) lamb, 1/2 leg and 1/2 shoulder, cut into chunks

seasoned flour for coating

1 large onion, coarsely chopped

1 red and 1 green pepper, seeded and coarsely chopped

4 cloves garlic, chopped

1/2 red chilli pepper, seeded and chopped

1¹/2 tsp hot smoked Spanish paprika (pimentón de la Vera)

1 tsp fresh thyme

1 tsp fresh rosemary

1 bay leaf

400ml (14fl oz) dry white wine

salt and pepper to taste

This dish reflects the fact that lamb is still king in many parts of northern Spain. The stew could easily be served as a main dish if the quantity were increased and potatoes served alongside it. Note the mixture of lamb cuts adds to the flavour and texture.

1 Heat the olive oil in a casserole. Dip the lamb chunks in flour, then brown them on all sides in the hot olive oil. Remove the lamb with a slotted spoon.

2 Put the onion, peppers, garlic and chilli in the casserole and cook in the same oil until tender.

3 Stir in the paprika, then add the lamb, herbs and white wine. Season and bring to the boil. Immediately turn the heat down very low, cover the pan, and cook the lamb gently for 1 - 1¹/4 hours, or until the meat is cooked through and very tender. Serve in a shallow earthenware dish.

Luis Benavente Bocaito, Madrid

Luis Benavente is one of a rare breed - a madrileño born and bred. At 14 years old he was washing plates in restaurants, his first rung on the ladder, and in 1966 he set up his own tapas bar. Since then, this 150-year-old bar in the once down-at-heel Chueca district has undergone renovation and twice expanded sideways - although the original Andaluz-style decoration has hardly changed. Here you will find beer from the barrel, suspended hams, marble floors and counters, signed photos of matadors, Andalucian tiles, nets of garlic and gigantic jars of olives. Through an open hatch to the kitchen you might spot Ana, Luis' youngest cook, flinging ingredients from huge ceramic pots into the relevant pan. All these features add to Bocaito's timeless atmosphere, something that is apparent in the extensive menu of tapas and raciones, which are largely traditional or regional specialities.

'Quality of basic ingredients is the most important thing,' says Luis, 'even if that means spending a little more money. From that point you move on, dressing up as little as possible.' Regulars flock here from the provinces for Luis' wide choice of seafood and 15 different egg dishes - a dying art in Madrid. Bocaito is one of the few remaining bars to serve freshly-made tortillas, omelettes and scrambled and fried eggs, whose popularity is testament to Luis' success in achieving his expressed aim: 'I want people to feel at home in my bar.'

Grilled lamb's kidneys
Riñones de cordero lechal plancha

for 6 tapas

500g (1¹/₈lb) lamb's kidneys, skinned and halved, plus their fat
salt and white pepper to taste
1 tbsp lemon juice

This is a classic case of the simpler a dish, the better it tastes. Buy the best quality lamb kidneys from your butcher, toss them in the frying pan and help to bring them back into fashion in succulent style.

1 Place the kidneys, cut-side-down, on a hot griddle and cook until golden. Turn, coat the kidneys protectively with their own fat, and continue to cook them slowly for about 10 minutes.

2 Season with salt and pepper and splash with lemon juice before serving.

Kidneys in sherry sauce
Riñones al jerez

for 6 tapas

olive oil for frying
500g (1¹/₈lb) lamb's kidneys, skinned and quartered
1 medium onion, thinly sliced
100ml (3¹/₂fl oz) dry sherry
salt and pepper to taste
1 tbsp finely chopped parsley
1 clove garlic, minced

This traditional southern Spanish dish is for those who like hard-hitting flavours – it needs a strong wine to complement them.

1 Pour a little oil into a frying pan, add the kidneys and sauté quickly so that they lose their strong aroma. Set the kidneys aside and discard any juices that have been drawn out of them.

2 In a different frying pan, fry the onion in a little olive oil until tender. Add the kidneys and sherry and season to taste. Cook until the kidneys are cooked through and the sherry sauce has reduced and thickened slightly.

3 Mound the coated kidneys on a plate and garnish with the chopped parsley and minced garlic.

'Quality of basic ingredients is the most important thing, even if that means spending a little more money. From that point you move on, dressing up as little as possible.'

Young garlic, broad bean and ham omelette
Tortilla de ajetes, habitas y jamón

for 4 tapas

50g (1³/₄oz) tender young garlic, minced
olive oil for frying
50g (1³/₄oz) small young broad beans, cooked
40g (1¹/₂oz) serrano ham, cut into thin strips
3 eggs, well beaten
salt and pepper to taste

This is a flavoursome twist on the classic Spanish potato *tortilla*, and should be served at room temperature.

1 In a medium-sized frying pan, sauté the garlic in a little olive oil until tender and golden. Add the beans and ham strips and stir to mix.

2 Add the eggs and seasoning and cook for 3-4 minutes, to form a firm but juicy omelette. Cool to room temperature, cut into triangular slices or squares and serve.

Avocado with smoked fish
Aguacate al humo

for 8 tapas
*4 avocados
2 lettuce hearts, cut into julienne strips
100ml (3¹/₂fl oz) mayonnaise
salt and white pepper to taste
50g (1³/₄oz) smoked salmon, cut into
thin strips
50g (1³/₄oz) smoked trout, cut into
thin strips
50g (1³/₄oz) smoked eel, cut into
thin strips
50g (1³/₄oz) smoked anchovy, cut into
thin strips
1 medium carrot, finely grated
6 tbsp extra virgin olive oil
1 tbsp white wine vinegar*

It's hard to avoid mayonnaise in Spain, but it's particularly important in this recipe as its texture complements the lettuce while its flavour is too subtle to fight with the smoked fish. Follow Luis Benavente's advice and buy the best quality products.

1 Halve the avocados and remove the stones. With a melon baller, form small balls of avocado and refill the avocado skins with them.

2 Mix the lettuce with the mayonnaise, salt and pepper, and spoon a generous amount over each avocado half.

3 Place several strips of each type of smoked fish over the lettuce mixture.

4 Mix the grated carrot with the olive oil and white wine vinegar and season with more salt and pepper. Arrange the avocado halves on a plate and drizzle generously with the vinaigrette.

Joaquín Campos Casa Matute, Madrid

In wry yet nonchalant style, Joaquín Campos hangs 'The 10 commandments of Casa Matute' outside his bar-restaurant near the Plaza Santa Ana. This is, in fact, his 10 recommended tapas and raciones – plus an 11th for good measure. Below it he quotes from songwriter Antonio Arias: 'Perfect contemplation means not knowing what you are looking at; he who doesn't know his destination accomplishes the perfect journey.' With its Buddhist connotations, this sums up Joaquín's gastronomic philosophy of spontaneous and fearless experimentation. Add to this another of his favourite dictums, 'Change is permanence,' and you have the key to his food and to his other great passion, cinema, as the phrase is borrowed from José Val del Omar, an avant-garde film-maker and poet of the 1930s. Indeed, for Joaquín, food has a cinematographic quality: colour, composition, action – and poetry.

Cultural chef he may be at heart, but Joaquín is clear about the practicalities of cooking too. 'I like mixing flavours – sweet and sour, for example – and contrasting strong flavours.' As a result, some of his dishes are so rich that your dining will stop right there, but with utter, lip-smacking satisfaction. Firing on all cylinders and a high dose of nervous energy, Joaquín is quick to point out the wines that best accompany each tapa, for the bar lines up more than 85 labels from all over Spain. 'I'm trying to encourage people to experiment,' he says.

Although only 27, Joaquín has passed through the kitchens of some of Madrid's top restaurants. He has swung pots and pans in Segovia and travelled in America and throughout the Mediterranean. This interest in travel is reflected in his menu: Norwegian herrings sit aside Italian provolone cheese. Quality and freshness of ingredients is king – there are vegetables from Andalucía alongside seafood from the Atlantic and Mediterranean. Somehow Joaquín's spirited and wide-ranging approach encapsulates the very energy of Madrid itself.

Baked tuna served with gingered rice
Ventresca de atún confitada con arroz à la crème de gingembre

for 4 tapas
15g (¹/₂oz) butter
¹/₂ tsp finely chopped fresh ginger
50g (1³/₄oz) long-grain rice
3 tbsp double cream
2 tbsp finely chopped parsley plus 1 tbsp for garnish
salt and white pepper to taste
250g (9oz) belly of tuna, skinned and filleted
2 tbsp finely chopped red onion
extra virgin olive oil

The tender fresh fish and sweet red onion are perfectly complemented by the delicate ginger flavour of the rice. It is essential to respect the baking time in order to preserve the flaky texture and colour of the tuna. The dish looks wonderful on a large platter or served in small, flat bowls. If the ingredients are multiplied, this tapa can equally well be served as a main course.

1 Melt the butter in a saucepan and sauté the ginger for about a minute. Add the rice, stir it around in the butter and ginger, and add 100ml (3½fl oz) water. Bring to the boil, turn the heat down low, cover and cook for about 15 minutes. The rice should be tender, but not totally soft, and the water should have evaporated. Stir in the cream, parsley, salt and pepper. Keep warm.

2 Preheat the oven to 170°C (325°F) Gas mark 3. Cut the tuna into four equal parts, then arrange it in a single layer in a lightly oiled oven-proof dish. Cover tightly with aluminium foil and place in the oven. Cook for 8 minutes.

3 Remove from the oven, salt lightly, and transfer to a serving plate. Arrange the pieces in a ring, leaving space in the centre for the rice. Sprinkle each piece of tuna with chopped onion and the remaining parsley. Finally, drizzle with extra virgin olive oil.

4 Spoon the creamy gingered rice into the centre of the plate and then serve immediately.

Iberian ham and broad bean salad
Habitas con jamón en concha de achicoria

for 4 tapas

200g (7oz) fresh broad beans or 150g (5oz) dried broad beans
1 large, very fresh radicchio leaf
olive oil for frying
2 cloves garlic, finely sliced
100g (3¹/₂oz) Iberian or serrano ham, thickly sliced and cut into thin strips
salt to taste
2 tsp finely chopped parsley

Pulses are big in central Spain, but in this recipe Joaquín Campos has chosen to limit their quantity while emphasising their visual appeal.

1 If using fresh broad beans, cook them in a little water for anything from 2-5 minutes, until tender (the younger they are the less cooking time they need). If using dried broad beans, soak them overnight, then cover them with fresh water and cook for 1-1¹/₂ hours, until tender. In both cases, once the beans have been drained and cooled slip them out of their skins.

2 Place the radicchio leaf in a container of iced water for about 15 minutes, until it brightens and stiffens.

3 Pour a little oil into a medium-sized frying pan. Add the garlic and cook slowly over a low heat until just golden. Add the ham strips, heat for 10 seconds, then add the broad beans. Season with salt to taste. Cook, stirring occasionally, until the beans are hot.

4 While the beans are frying, remove the radicchio leaf from the iced water, pat it dry and place it on a serving plate. Fill the leaf with the beans, allowing some to overflow on to the plate. Sprinkle with parsley and serve.

Duck liver in sherry
Foie fresco al Pedro Ximénez

for 4 tapas

225ml (8fl oz) sweet Pedro Ximénez sherry
300g (10¹/₂oz) fresh duck's livers, cut into 4 thin slices
salt to taste

Duck's liver has a smooth, light texture and a stronger flavour than chicken's liver, but you can use the latter for this dish if you prefer. With the simple addition of this sweet sherry sauce, it makes an unusual and extremely rich tapa or starter with strong echoes of Andalucía. This recipe is quick to make and quick to serve.

1 Prepare the sauce by cooking the sherry over a very high heat until it begins to foam. Reduce the liquid until it is thick and sticky. Remove from the heat.

2 Quickly fry the liver slices in a hot ungreased skillet for about 1 minute on each side, until sealed and slightly brown. Transfer to a serving plate, pour on the sherry sauce and sprinkle with salt. Serve immediately.

Fried goat's cheese with honey
Queso de cabra frito con miel

for 4 tapas

*3 medium sweet red onions,
very finely sliced*

olive oil for frying

50g (1³/₄oz) sugar

150g (5¹/₂oz) cylindrical goat's cheese

1 egg, beaten

flour

2 tbsp liquid honey

1 tbsp finely chopped parsley

2 chive stalks

This is an exquisite, though rich, *nueva cocina* tapa. The hot goat's cheese is a delicious match for the cold caramelised onions. The honey should not be too highly flavoured, as this would drown the more subtle cheese, and it must be liquid so that it drizzles easily. The parsley is optional, but adds a splash of colour to this minimalist plate.

1 Prepare the garnish several hours before serving. Fry the onions in 3 tbsp oil over a low heat until they are really soft – it will take about 20 minutes. Drain off the excess oil and add the sugar. Stir until the sugar and onion are blended and the sugar has caramelised (about 8 minutes). Cool and refrigerate.

2 About 30 minutes before serving, form four perfect equal-sized balls of goat's cheese. Dip in the egg and then flour and fry in just enough oil to cover the bottom of the pan – turning carefully to lightly brown all sides. Drain on a paper towel.

3 Put the caramelised onions in the centre of a serving plate, and evenly space the fried cheese balls around it. Drizzle with honey, then sprinkle parsley over the top and add a criss-cross of chives. Serve at once.

José Luis Ruiz Solaguren   José Luis, Madrid

The recognised king of Madrid tapas is José Luis Ruiz Solaguren, a Basque who started his working life as a shoe-shiner in a Bilbao café some 60 years ago and who now heads an international chain of tapas bars and restaurants. His gastro-kingdom not only spans three venues in Madrid, but also nets Montreal, Miami and Mexico City – and has recently tacked on a vineyard and bodega in Castile. The secret of his success? 'My mother was a cook and my father a taxi-driver, so I grew up with the notions of good food and service,' he explains, a fact that is immediately apparent in his hands-on approach. Even at the age of 74 and with two sons running the business, this dapper, expressive man still loves to preside over the comings and goings of his regulars, stopping to chat or leading customers to a table at his latest restaurant in Madrid's grandiose Teatro Real (Royal Theatre).

José Luis' classic menu at the flagship tapas bar in Calle Serrano offers a dazzling range of hot and cold tapas, pinchos and raciones. These are good, unpretentious interpretations of Spanish classics, slickly presented. According to José Luis, 'As tapas means eating in a varied way, you can try all sorts of things, mixing different colours and textures. But the most important thing in cooking is having an appetite.' It is a philosophy that remains true to his modest origins – and he continues the tradition of resident shoe-shiners in his bars!

Cured ham and green pepper on toast
Jamón ibérico con pimiento

for 4 tapas
4 slices French bread
1 tbsp olive oil
1 green pepper, sliced
4 slices jamón ibérico cured ham

José Luis serves many simple but classic tapas – and this is one of them. Be sure to use the best quality ham, as the simplicity of this dish means it depends on delicious ingredients.

1 Lightly toast the slices of French bread on each side until golden.

2 Heat the olive oil in a frying pan. Quickly fry the green pepper slices.

3 Put a piece of ham on each toast, shaping it to fit. Then position the pepper strips on top.

Anchovy with sheep's cheese on toast
Anchoa con queso

for 4 tapas
4 slices French bread
4 slices sheep's cheese
4 anchovy fillets

A wonderfully salty tapa – the sheep's cheese and anchovy combine to create a powerful flavour. Ideal as an appetiser.

1 Lightly toast the slices of French bread on each side until golden.

2 Lay a slice of sheep's cheese on each toast, and then top with an anchovy fillet.

Organic cured beef, caviar or smoked salmon on toast
Lomo ibérico de bellota, kaviar o Salmón ahumado

for 12 tapas
12 slices French bread
4 slices cured beef
120g (4oz) lumpfish roe
4 slices smoked salmon

José Luis is passionate about simple, good food. These are more ideas than recipes, but they make luxuriously simple snacks and look great on a plate together.

1 Lightly toast the slices of French bread on each side until golden.

2 Lay slices of the best quality cured beef on four toasts, a heaped spoonful of lumpfish roe on a further four and a slice of smoked salmon on the final four.

Smoked fish tartare
Tartar de ahumados

for 4 tapas
50g (1³/4oz) smoked anchovies,
finely chopped
50g (1³/4oz) smoked salmon,
finely chopped
50g (1³/4oz) smoked trout,
finely chopped
2 tsp diced onion
2 tsp diced capers
75g (2³/4oz) mayonnaise
4 slices French bread

A delicious combination of three smoked fish, this is another salty tapa that makes a fabulous appetiser. The onion and capers add a piquancy that will really get your juices flowing.

1 Lightly toast the French bread on each side.

2 Mix the smoked anchovies, salmon and trout together. Add the diced onion and capers and mayonnaise.

3 Heap a large spoonful of the paste on to each slice of toast.

'As tapas means eating in a varied way, you can try all sorts of things, mixing different colours and textures. But the most important thing in cooking is having an appetite.'

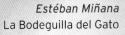

Estéban Miñana
La Bodeguilla del Gato

Colin Ward
Gambrinus

Emiliano García Domene
Bodega Montaña

Michele Gallana
Santa Companya

Raquel Sabater
Mesón de Labradores

'*T*he land where the east wind blows': this is Spain's Levante and the phrase carries a revealing echo of the region's gastronomic influences from the Middle East. Between the beaches and the herb-studded sierra, this Mediterranean coastal region produces an astonishingly abundant and diverse range of food.

Not quite milk and honey - more rice and oranges – the Levante's produce encompasses glistening fish, almonds, cherries, grapes, grapefruits, lemons, loquats, artichokes, black truffles, dates and, yes, honey. Rich soil, a temperate climate and a history of multifarious agricultural influences give the region the

protracted family get-together every Sunday. Alongside the fragrant, saffron-imbibed amalgam of chicken, prawns, vegetables and rice (a dish that has sadly suffered an abusive, tourist-oriented fate), *paella's* many variations may combine *bacalao* with spinach or rabbit with seafood, and may include either small game, turkey or sausage meats. And, despite *paella's* association with gargantuan proportions, the dish is sometimes spooned out at bars in tapa-sized portions - both in the Levante and in other regions of Spain.

The heart and soul of any *paella* is, of course, rice, although even this is

'*Not quite milk and honey – more rice and oranges – the Levante's produce encompasses glistening fish, almonds, cherries, grapes, grapefruits, lemons, loquats, artichokes, black truffles, dates and, yes, honey.*'

reputation of being the most fertile in the whole of Europe. This, along with the Levante's ability to attract a rather cosmopolitan population, is the key influence behind the area's 'new' tapas.

Paella, Spain's national dish, was born near Valencia, the Levante's main city, barely two centuries ago. As is often the case with dishes that make such imaginative use of some basic ingredients, *paella* evolved from the poor man's needs, combining tasty leftovers into a body-building lunch that, conveniently, could be prepared outdoors over an open fire.

The tradition of never eating *paella* in the evening continues, *digestion oblige*, but more often than not this dish is now consumed in restaurants during a

sometimes replaced by *fideos* (fine noodles that will absorb squid ink, saffron or fish juices). Rice, whether grains of *bomba*, *granza* or *secreti*, was first cultivated here by the Moors during their 500-year rule over the region, and paddy fields still blanket the marshes surrounding the Albufera lagoon south of Valencia. Evidence of the grain's versatility and inspirational role in the local cooking is that one restaurant situated in Alicante features as many as 70 rice dishes on its menu.

Before the Moors, the equally long Roman occupancy left a taste in this region for seafood preserved in brine or salt, while waves of Jewish settlers brought with them luscious Middle Eastern gastronomic influences. Further back still, salt was produced by the Iberians in the salt-marshes of Murcia to the south and the palm grove at Elche – now Europe's largest, numbering as many as 125,000 date palms – is thought to have been planted by the Phoenicians.

The Italian influence upon food, art and architecture returned in the 15th and 16th centuries, when Spain's eastern seaboard governed Naples and Sicily. But the Levante's resultant mercantile glory foundered once the Moriscos (Moors converted to Christianity) and Jews were turned out in 1609. With this exodus of both traders and skilled farmers, the backbone of agriculture in the region fell apart, to be revived only in more recent years.

One major spin-off of the Levante's abundance is that the diet enjoyed in the area is arguably the most balanced in all of Spain. Fish is the mainstay, along with rice *a banda* (cooked in fish broth and then served separately), and heaps of roasted vegetables (*escalibada*) which are liberally doused in olive oil, followed by the juiciest possible seasonal fruit. Valencian sweets reflect the region's Arab influence, with *horchata* (a cold drink made from the *chufa* or tiger-nut, a peanut-sized tuber), almonds, honey and candied fruit cakes, marzipan and *turrón* (nougat) all ubiquitous.

In cultural terms, contemporary Valencia is speeding swiftly ahead, incorporating flashes of designer chic into a city of stunning Renaissance buildings whose towering cathedral claims to possess the Holy Grail, no less. As the Valencian identity strengthens, its protagonists separate themselves increasingly from their Catalan cousins to the north of the country – people who, although speaking a similar language to the Valencians, have notable historical and social differences.

You can sense the ongoing renewal in Valencia as you wander through grandiose squares lined with renovated mansions; enter a converted convent that is now a contemporary arts centre, or survey the expanding forms of Santiago Calatrava's ambitious City of Arts and Sciences. The growing cosmopolitanism is evident on a more basic level, for here you can sip a good Australian wine while enjoying an Italian tapa in one of the city's ever-increasing number of specialist tapas bars.

As with Catalonia, the tapas tradition is not as deeply embedded in Valencia as it is in Madrid, Andalucía or the Basque country. However, in the narrow streets of the old quarter of Valencia, entrepreneurial young chefs from Bilbao, Venice or London are setting a different tone for this metamorphosing city. It would not be difficult to bet that, within just a few years, Valencia will vie with Barcelona and Madrid as a hot destination for food-lovers.

Despite these changes, there remains something touchingly Old World about Valencia, whether in the last decoratively peeling façades, in the shops overflowing with *mantillas* (scarves), fans and embroidered shawls, in a tiled bar with neon tubes artfully inserted into an ageing chandelier or in the succulent anchovies that are sold by the single fillet.

Above all, the magnificent iron and glass creation that is the 75-year-old *Mercado Central*, one of Europe's most picturesque and diverse municipal markets, paints the true picture of the Levante's gastronomic riches. Valencia is not globalised (yet); it is human – for the moment, at any rate. Follow this region's example by concentrating on astute combinations of ultra-fresh ingredients and your taste-buds, as well as your constitution, will be grateful.

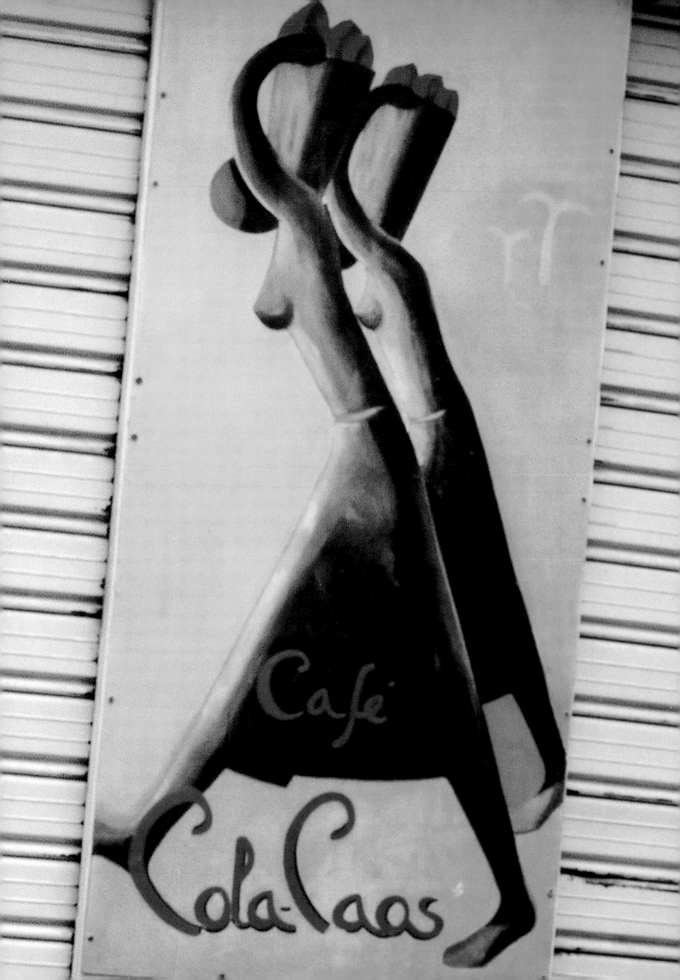

Estéban Miñana   La Bodeguilla del Gato, Valencia

Located in the heart of El Carmen, a hot nocturnal quarter (hence 'Gato', or 'cat', which refers to the late-night habits of the madrileños), this tapas bar brings with it influences and traditions from northern Spain. On the menu, developed by the chef Estéban Miñana and owners Pepe Lopez and Andres Canelas, are tapas that wouldn't look amiss in Bilbao or Madrid, the origins of the trio.

Estéban notes that there is a big difference in tapas eating habits in the north and south of Spain. 'Here people tend to sit and eat, drinking cocktails or beer, whereas in the north they move around from bar to bar drinking copas of wine. It means that tapas has actually become a meal here,' he explains. Estéban's first career, as an industrial designer, also influences his tapas. 'Food and design are both about a mixture of colours and lines,' he explains. 'Taste is, of course, important, but appearance counts too.' Make no mistake, though – Estéban's unpretentious classics are full of flavour.

Only open in the evenings, La Bodeguilla del Gato packs in its ravenous customers between brick walls hung with contemporary paintings, photographs of bull-fighting and concert posters. Despite – or perhaps because of – their northern influence, Estéban's tapas obviously appeal to local appetites.

Fishermen's mussels
Mejillones à la marinera

for 6 tapas

750g (1lb 10oz) fresh mussels, scrubbed, any that remain open discarded

75ml (2¹/₂ fl oz) dry white wine

1 bay leaf

2 tbsp olive oil

1 large onion, finely chopped

1 red pepper, finely chopped

1 green pepper, finely chopped

2 cloves garlic, minced

2 ripe tomatoes, finely chopped

¹/₈ tsp cayenne pepper

white pepper to taste

Choose large, plump mussels to complement the generous tomato sauce, with its aromatic echoes of the Mediterranean.

1 Place the mussels in a large pot with the wine and bay leaf and cook, covered, over a high heat for a few minutes, shaking occasionally until the shells open. Remove to a serving platter, discarding any mussels whose shells have not opened, and keep warm. Reserve the cooking liquid.

2 Heat the olive oil in a saucepan. Sauté the onion, peppers and garlic until tender. Add the tomatoes and cayenne pepper and cook for about 15 minutes, until the mixture is thick. Stir in a little of the cooking liquid from the mussels and season with white pepper.

3 Pour the sauce over the mussels and serve at once.

Spicy sausage in red wine
Chorizo al vino

for 4 tapas

550g (1¹/4lb) semi-cured chorizo or other spicy sausage
350ml (12fl oz) dry red wine
1 bay leaf

In the north of Spain, chorizo is often cooked in cider. Estéban prefers to adapt the recipe, using red wine instead of cider, to create a warmer dish. This makes an excellent wintry tapa to accompany glasses of good Rioja.

1 Place the sausage in a frying pan with the wine and bay leaf. Cover and cook over a low heat for 10-15 minutes, or until the wine has slightly reduced.

2 Remove the sausage from the pan and cut it into 1cm (¹/2-inch) slices. Return the slices to the wine and stir. Serve in individual earthenware dishes with chunks of French bread.

Squid in a tomato and garlic sauce
Calamar encebollada

for 4 tapas

700g (1lb 9oz) squid, cleaned, prepared and cut into 2.5cm (1-inch) pieces
100ml (3¹/2fl oz) water
1 bay leaf
4 cloves garlic, thinly sliced
olive oil for frying
1 large onion, thinly sliced in rings
1 ripe tomato, finely chopped
¹/2 tbsp sweet paprika
150ml (¹/4-pint) white wine or 75ml (3fl oz) glass Cognac
salt and pepper to taste

This is a classic Mediterranean dish, combining squid with some of the region's favourite ingredients: tomatoes, onions, garlic and bay. Use Cognac instead of white wine for a more intense sauce.

1 Place the squid in a heavy cooking pot with the water and bay leaf. Bring to the boil and boil for 3 minutes, while constantly stirring to separate the squid. Remove from the pot and set aside. Reserve the cooking liquid.

2 Sauté the garlic in a little olive oil until tender. Add another 2 tbsp of olive oil and the onion rings, cover and cook over a low heat for about 20 minutes.

3 Add the tomato, paprika, white wine or Cognac, salt and pepper. Cook slowly, uncovered, until the sauce is quite thick. Add the squid and some of the cooking liquid to the sauce and stir to mix well. Serve immediately.

SEPIA

250 Ptas 1/4 Kg

Colin Ward   Gambrinus, Valencia

This could be the joker in our pack. A Londoner held up as an exemplary conjuror of tapas?
Yet somehow Gambrinus - situated in Plaza de la Reina, Valencia's most illustrious square
- is quintessentially Spanish. It nets large family groups for Sunday paella and a constant
flow during the rest of the week for its succulent tapas. In the summer, the overflow is
accommodated by pavement tables from which diners can muse on the Gothic cathedral, its
octagonal bell-tower and the truth behind its Holy Grail.

The success of Gambrinus' food owes much to chef Colin Ward's Andalucian adolescence
when, between fruit-picking, cultivating his own vegetable patch and dodging errant
donkeys, he developed a passion for all things Spanish. 'When I went back to London I became
a singer in a band that came to Valencia for a few gigs. Then I met my Mallorcan wife, and
so the dye was cast and we came here to live,' he recounts. Colin has since mastered
a repertoire of Valencian dishes and tapas that no local chef could criticise. 'In the end
Valencian food is all about fresh ingredients, and the local pork and chicken are particularly
good. You don't need sauces to hide anything as the basic flavours are all there,' he says.

There's a personal angle to at least one of Colin's dishes, too: 'The Pica-pica recipe I learnt
from my wife, who learnt it from her grandmother,' he explains.

Tarragon chicken with asparagus
Pollo al estragón

for 4 tapas
60g (2¹/₄oz) butter
1 medium onion, finely chopped
250g (9oz) chicken breast, cut into
2.5cm (1-inch) cubes
55g (2oz) fresh tarragon, leaves
removed and chopped
4 tbsp flour
350ml (12fl oz) milk
8 stalks fresh asparagus, peeled and
coarsely chopped
salt and pepper to taste

Asparagus grows prolifically in Valencia, but while this ingredient may be traditional, milk – a food rarely seen in Spanish cooking – is more English. But then this is cosmopolitan Valencia, so why not?

1 Melt the butter in a large frying pan. Add the onion and chicken and cook, stirring frequently, until the onion is tender and the chicken is lightly browned. Add the tarragon and flour and cook gently, stirring until everthing is well mixed together. Take the pan off the heat and slowly add the milk, making sure that you blend in each addition before adding more.
Put the pan back on the heat and bring to the boil, stirring constantly, until the mixture has thickened and is smooth and creamy.

2 Turn the heat down, add the asparagus, salt and pepper and simmer for 5 minutes, or until the chicken is cooked through. Serve hot in individual earthenware dishes.

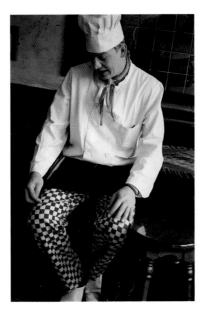

Marinated mackerel with roasted vegetables
Escalibada con caballa en escabeche

for 6 tapas

1 aubergine, halved lengthways
1 courgette, halved lengthways
1 onion, peeled and quartered
1 red pepper, halved and seeded
1 fennel bulb, trimmed, quartered and central heart removed
olive oil for roasting
ground rock salt to taste
100ml (3½fl oz) dry white wine
200ml (7fl oz) olive oil
4 mackerel fillets, cleaned and prepared
6 cloves
4 cloves garlic, unpeeled
4 bay leaves

Escalibada is an eastern Spanish classic that makes full use of the abundant fresh vegetables grown locally. The name comes from the Catalan word for 'charred', and ideally the vegetables should be cooked over a barbecue to get a really full, smoky flavour. *Escalibada* can be served with any kind of preserved or marinated fish, though mackerel work perfectly.

1 Place the vegetables (except for the garlic) cut-side-down on a baking sheet, brush with olive oil, season with rock salt and roast at 200ºC (400ºF) Gas mark 6 for 35 minutes.

2 To prepare the marinade, whisk together the wine and olive oil. Put the mackerel fillets in a wide saucepan and pour over just enough marinade to cover them. Add the cloves, garlic and bay, cover the saucepan, and simmer for 15 minutes.

3 Peel the skin from the roast pepper halves and cut the stem off the aubergine halves. Slice the vegetables thinly and arrange in the centre of a plate. Place the mackerel fillets on top of the vegetables and garnish the rim of the plate with the bay leaves and garlic cloves. This tapa can be served warm or cool, but not refrigerated.

Squid in a tomato, garlic and red wine sauce
Calamares pica-pica

for 4 tapas

100ml (3¹/₂fl oz) olive oil
500g (1lb 2oz) squid, cleaned, prepared
and cut into 5cm (2-inch) pieces
1 onion, coarsely chopped
200g (7oz) tomatoes, coarsely chopped
2 cloves garlic, crushed
1 red pepper, seeded and chopped
1 bay leaf
200ml (7fl oz) red wine
100ml (3¹/₂fl oz) fish stock

Easy to make yet oozing with flavour, this Mallorcan tapa is a real hit in Valencia. Make sure the squid you use is small and tender.

1 Heat the olive oil in a large saucepan. Add the squid and stir-fry for 1 minute. Add the onion and tomatoes and fry for 5 more minutes.

2 Add the garlic, pepper, bay leaf, red wine and stock, stir and then simmer for 20 minutes. Serve hot in earthenware dishes, with crusty bread.

Cod, spinach and tomato paella
Paella de bacalao y espinacas

for 6 tapas

500g (1lb 2oz) fresh spinach, washed and destalked
4 tbsp olive oil
150g (5¹/₂oz) salt cod, desalted (see page 135) and flesh cut into strips
30g (1¹/₄oz) pine nuts
250g (9oz) tomatoes, chopped
2 cloves garlic, crushed
2 tsp sweet paprika
1 dried chilli pepper, chopped
250g (9oz) Calasparra rice
500ml (18fl oz) vegetable stock
¹/₂ tsp saffron threads, infused in 2 tbsp just boiled water for 15 minutes
salt to taste
lemon wedges to serve

Of the myriad forms of *paella*, this is one of the most delicious, with its distinctive flavour and dark colour. You can replace the salt cod with fresh cod or hake, but do try to get small, round-grained Spanish Calasparra rice.

1 Cook the spinach, in the water left on the leaves after washing, in a covered pan over a medium heat for 4 minutes. Squeeze out the excess water and chop.

2 Heat the olive oil in a 60cm (24-inch) *paella* pan or large frying pan. When very hot, add the cod, spinach, pine nuts, tomatoes, garlic, paprika and dried chilli. Lower the heat and cook, stirring constantly, for 6 minutes.

3 Add the rice and continue to cook, while stirring, for 2 more minutes. Add the stock and saffron. Season with salt and simmer for about 15 minutes, or until the stock has been absorbed and the rice is just tender.

4 Remove from the heat, cover with a tea-towel, put the lid on, and allow to stand for 5 minutes. Garnish with lemon wedges and serve at once.

Emiliano García Domene   Bodega Montaña, Valencia

The Mediterranean sea plays a key role in the tapas at Bodega Montaña, not least because the bar lies a few blocks from the waves in El Cabañal, the fishermen's quarter on the outskirts of Valencia. Despite its far-flung location, Bodega Montaña's well-worn features (it dates from 1836), its list of over 900 wines and its succulent tapas ensure it is known by every tapa-hopper in the city. Surveying and serving them all is Vicente, the well-disposed manager.

From its modest early days as a general store, Bodega Montaña blossomed under the 45-year-long ownership of a Frenchman who introduced wine, olive oils and finally tapas. When Emiliano García Domene took over in the early 1990s, he introduced wines from Italy, Argentina, Chile, New Zealand, Australia and South Africa to accompany the stocks of Rioja and Valdepeñas. For Spain - and even more so for Valencia - this was a brave step.

And the tapas? Again concentrating on quality products but respecting local tastes, the menu offers the classics, a wide variety of specialist sausage meats and hams and a string of seafood delicacies. Premium anchovy fillets are sold individually, while Valencian mussels (clochinas), sardines, squid and octopus are the standard delectable fare.

Potato, salt cod and garlic mash
Bacalao al ajo arriero

for 6 tapas
250g (9oz) salt cod
500g (1lb 2oz) peeled potatoes
3 hard-boiled egg yolks, chopped
4 large cloves garlic, finely chopped
100ml (3¹/₂fl oz) olive oil

This delicious little tapa is served as a dip, packed into tiny dishes with a bread-stick pushed into one end. It's an easy, basic dish which your guests will devour. The quantities below are generous, catering for fishermen's appetites.

1 Soak the salt cod in water for 2 days, changing the water a couple of times a day. Rinse. Flake the flesh, leaving any bones and skin behind.

2 Boil the potatoes until they are just soft. Remove from the heat, drain and then mash them. Once they are mashed, beat them with a wooden spoon to ensure they are smooth.

3 Add the egg yolks, garlic and salt cod. Mix well, and continue to beat briskly while slowly adding the olive oil. Beat until you have a smooth, thick purée.

Deep-fried red piquillo peppers with a tuna stuffing
Pimientos del piquillo rellenos

for 4 tapas

*8 whole red piquillo peppers, fresh or
canned, or 4 ordinary red peppers*

50g (1oz) butter

1 tbsp sunflower oil

30g (1oz) plain flour

10g (1/4oz) cornflour

300ml (1/2 pint) milk

salt and pepper to taste

freshly grated nutmeg to taste

*150g (51/2oz) tinned tuna in oil, drained
and flaked*

beaten egg for coating

flour for coating

olive or sunflower oil for frying

Although *piquillo* peppers are grown in Navarra and Rioja, they are in demand throughout the peninsula for their concentrated juiciness and sweetness. If you can't find fresh ones, use the tinned variety.

1 If you are using fresh peppers rather than tinned, halve and seed them and then grill them until blistered and black in places. Cool and then peel off the skins.

2 To prepare the stuffing, make a white sauce by melting the butter in a pan with the oil. Add the flour and cornflour, stirring constantly until the flours and fats have come together and you have a roux. Cook until the roux is pale gold in colour, then remove from the heat. Add the milk, a little at a time, making sure each addition is incorporated into the roux before you add the next bit. Put the pan back on the heat and bring to the boil, stirring continuously to obtain a smooth sauce. Cook over a low heat, stirring from time to time, for 5 minutes.

3 Take the sauce off the heat and season well with salt, pepper and nutmeg. Add the tuna, mix, and then allow to cool. Refrigerate for 12 hours.

4 About half an hour before serving, fill the peppers with the tuna mixture, taking care not to tear them. Fold the peppers over the filling. Dip them in the egg and then flour and carefully lower them into about 10cm (4 inches) hot oil. Fry until lightly browned on all sides. Drain them on paper towels and serve immediately.

Artichoke hearts with black olive oil
Alcachofa con aceite de oliva negra

for 8 tapas
100g (3¹/₂oz) pitted black olives
200ml (7fl oz) extra virgin olive oil
8 artichoke hearts, cooked, or canned and well drained

Bar Montaña has produced an ultra-simple recipe here which is light, delicious and yet looks like a work of art.

1 Prepare the black olive oil by mixing the olives and oil in a blender until the olives are finely chopped.

2 Just before serving, place the artichoke hearts on a plate and pour the black olive oil over them.

Spicy broad bean and pork stew
Habas condimentadas

for 6 tapas
500g (1lb 2oz) dried broad beans, soaked for 48 hours
30g (1¹/₄oz) lomo Ibérico (cured pork loin)
30g (1¹/₄oz) cured beef
50g (1³/₄oz) chorizo or other spicy sausage
10g (¹/₄oz) smoked ham
1 small ham bone
125g (4¹/₂oz) chistorra or pork sausage
30g (1¹/₄oz) fresh mint leaves
6 bay leaves
1 tsp cayenne pepper
1.4 litres (2¹/₂ pints) chicken stock or water
4 tbsp olive oil
25g (1oz) hot smoked Spanish paprika (pimentón de la Vera)
salt and pepper to taste

Typical of southern Spanish 'peasant' food, this tapa contrasts the satisfying earthiness of pork and other meats with the mellow broad beans - a pulse that definitely deserves a revival.

1 Place all the ingredients except the olive oil, paprika, salt and pepper, in a large saucepan - in the order in which they appear in the ingredients list - using just enough stock or water to cover the rest of the ingredients.

2 Heat the olive oil in a little frying pan, add the paprika and stir to blend. Pour this over the bean mixture, cover the pan and place over a high heat. When the mixture comes to the boil, turn the heat down and cook everything slowly for 1¹/₂-2 hours, or until the beans are tender. Top up the stock from time to time if necessary.

3 Remove the ham bone. Season the stew with salt and pepper (adding salt before this stage would make the beans hard) and serve hot in individual earthenware dishes.

Michele Gallana   Santa Companya, Valencia

Foodies beware - this hip bar, hidden in central Valencia's maze of narrow streets, is breaking new fusion ground. And that's fusion in the Mediterranean, as opposed to East-West, sense. Santa Companya was opened in 2001 by a young Italian architect, Michele Gallana, two sleeping partners, both of whom are Italian, and a Valencian architect who designed the bar. All the tapas and raciones are prepared at a tiny counter behind the bar, where much attention is paid to presentation. The bar only serves chilled dishes, from open sandwiches (montaditos) of European cheeses (Gorgonzola, St Nectaire, Stilton, Munster) with honey, marmalade or quince paste, to tapas based on Spanish and Italian sausage-meats, Galician seafood preserves or epicurean salads. Loaves and fishes eat your heart out; Italian savoir-faire has hit town.

Michele hails from the Veneto. 'My grandmother had a restaurant that I often went to as a child,' he says. 'We opened this wine bar to serve top-quality European wines,' he continues. Food was not the priority, but the momentum grew and customers now come as much for the ricotta or Parma ham as for a bottle of Rioja. 'Valencians stay longer in bars than people elsewhere in Spain - they order a bottle, not a glass, and they sit,' he says. This seems to be an excellent reason for imitating Santa Companya's success by following his recipes.

Ostrich carpaccio
Carpaccio de avestruz

for 4 tapas

200g (7oz) ostrich fillets, cooked and cut into paper-thin slices
125ml (4fl oz) olive oil for the marinade
several fresh mint leaves
peel from 1 mandarin orange, cut into small pieces
75g (2³/₄oz) wholegrain Dijon mustard
juice of ¹/₂ orange
1-2 tbsp olive oil for the sauce
salt and pepper to taste
6 drops 8-year-old balsamic vinegar
2 tbsp almond slivers
2 tbsp pine nuts

Although Michele developed this recipe for ostrich meat, it is equally good with beef. The virtually transparent slices of meat easily absorb the tangy orange and mint flavours. This, combined with the flavours of mustard and balsamic vinegar, makes a highly aromatic and easily devoured tapa.

1 Macerate the ostrich in the olive oil, mint leaves and orange peel for 1 hour.

2 For the sauce, mix the mustard, orange juice, olive oil, salt and pepper.

3 Remove the meat from the marinade and arrange it on a platter. Cover with the sauce, splash with the vinegar and garnish with the almond slivers and pine nuts.

Spicy steak tartare
Bistec tartar de Michele

for 6 tapas
4 tbsp finely chopped parsley
4 mild chilli peppers, seeded and finely chopped
1 small onion, finely chopped
50g (1³/₄oz) capers, rinsed of vinegar, brine or salt
500g (1lb 2oz) sirloin steak, minced
6 drops Tabasco sauce
salt and pepper to taste
extra virgin olive oil to taste
60g (2¹/₄oz) Dijon herb mustard

The palate is under a happy assault from this spicy tapa, with its onion, chilli peppers, capers and Tabasco.

1 In a bowl, mix together the parsley, chilli peppers, onion and capers. Add the minced sirloin and mix well.

2 Sprinkle with Tabasco, salt, pepper and oil to taste and mix to combine all the ingredients. Mound on a platter or on individual plates and serve with the herb mustard.

Marinated sardines with onions in sherry
Sarde en saor

for 6 tapas
500g (1lb 2oz) small fresh sardines, gutted and scaled
flour for coating
olive oil for frying
4 onions, finely chopped
125ml (4fl oz) white wine vinegar
salt and pepper to taste

Michele learnt this traditional Venetian seamen's way of marinating sardines from his grandmother. To give it a Valencian touch, mix in a handful of pine nuts and raisins just before serving.

1 Coat the sardines with flour and fry them in a thin layer of hot oil until they are delicately browned on both sides. Drain on paper towels.

2 In a separate pan, slowly fry the onions in oil until they are golden. Remove from the heat, add the vinegar and seasoning and stir well.

3 Alternate layers of sardines and onions in a deep dish, beginning with sardines and ending with the onions. Cool and refrigerate for at least 2 hours.

4 To serve, spoon generous portions on to individual plates.

Cheese and quince
Queso con membrillo

for 6 tapas
6 slices Manchego cheese
3 slices country bread
quince paste

Saltiness and sweetness combine in this traditional Spanish tapa. Michele experiments using different cheeses, including *queso de tetilla*, an obscure spherical cow's cheese from Galicia, but ultimately little can beat the satisfying tanginess of Manchego.

1 Lay a piece of Manchego cheese on a half-slice of country bread.

2 Place a smaller wedge of quince paste on top of the cheese.

'Valencians stay longer in bars than people elsewhere in Spain - they order a bottle, not a glass, and they sit.'

Raquel Sabater   Mesón de Labradores, Alicante

If you ask an older Alicantino the way to Mesón de Labradores, he might just tell you how, in his rebel-rousing youth, that was where he spent his evenings out. Tapas bars come and go in this port town, which is also a crossroads for tourists on their way to the beaches of the Costa Blanca, but Labradores is a permanent fixture. Now, under the guidance of Raquel Sabàter, the founder's grand-daughter, it serves up tapas to 300 people nightly in a street once lined with bars and restaurants.

The bar's rustic style was the work of Raquel's grandfather, an antique restorer from Murcia. Copper pans, half-tiled walls, lampshades of dried garlic bulbs and leather-seated chairs all give a timeless atmosphere that is echoed by the menu. 'Most of our recipes are traditional, and hardly vary,' says Raquel. 'The only one we won't reveal is the Chupi chupi' – at which point she licks her fingers to illustrate the meaning of the word. 'That's basically a superior open sandwich of good country bread made with beef and a special sauce. My father tasted it in Barcelona, developed the recipe and it became the house speciality.' Although the wind of change has yet to whistle through Labradores, its recipes represent the gastro-soul of this good-natured corner of Spain.

Spicy pork kebabs
Pinchos morunos

for 4 tapas
3 tbsp olive oil
2 tbsp white wine vinegar
$1/4$ tsp ground cumin
$1/4$ tsp sweet Spanish paprika
$1/4$ tsp hot Spanish paprika
2 tbsp chopped parsley
2 cloves garlic, minced
500g (1lb 2oz) lean pork, cut in 2.5cm (1-inch) cubes
4 wooden or metal skewers
salt and pepper to taste

The name of these popular meat kebabs, '*morunos*', means 'Moorish' and, to make an obvious pun, they are certainly 'moreish'. Use good-quality pork (a southern Spanish substitute for the Moors' lamb), preferably organic, in order to make tender, highly-flavoured kebabs. They are ideally cooked on a barbecue, but taste fine cooked on a standard grill.

1 Prepare a marinade by mixing all the ingredients except for the pork cubes and salt and pepper.

2 Pour the marinade over the pork cubes and leave for 48 hours.

3 Thread the pork on to the skewers and grill on a high heat for 4-5 minutes on each side, until all sides are brown. Sprinkle with salt and pepper and serve at once.

Broad bean, ham and sausage stew
Michirones a la murciana

for 6 tapas
500g (1lb 2oz) dried broad beans,
soaked for 48 hours
125g (4¹/₂oz) chorizo or other spicy
sausage, cut in 1.25cm (¹/₂-inch) slices
100g (3¹/₂oz) serrano ham, thickly cut
and diced
1 ham bone
2 dried red chilli peppers,
finely chopped
1.4 litres (2¹/₂ pints) beef stock
salt to taste

This is one of Labradores' most popular tapas. The recipe originates in Murcia, Spain's smallest autonomous region, which lies between Valencia and Andalucía. It is similar to the Spicy broad bean and pork stew from Bodega Montaña, but the beef stock makes this a meatier dish.

1 Place all the ingredients in a large saucepan - in the order in which they appear in the ingredients list - using just enough stock to cover. But don't add any salt and pepper yet.

2 Cover the pan and place over a high heat. When the mixture comes to the boil, turn the heat down and cook everything slowly for 1¹/₂-2 hours, or until the beans are tender. Top up the stock from time to time if necessary.

3 Remove the ham bone. Season with salt and pepper (adding salt before this stage would make the beans hard) and serve hot in individual earthenware dishes with chunks of French bread or a few bread sticks.

Poor man´s potatoes
Patatas al pobre

for 6 tapas
10 tbsp olive oil for frying
2 large Spanish onions, sliced into rings
6 medium-sized firm potatoes, peeled and sliced
salt to taste
1 tbsp sherry vinegar
3 cloves garlic, minced

There are endless variants to this recipe in southern Spain, some of which include red or green peppers. If you want to incorporate peppers, they should be seeded and sliced and added immediately after the onion and before the potatoes.

1 In a heavy skillet, heat 2 tbsp oil and fry the onions for 10 minutes, stirring occasionally, until they are golden.

2 Add the remaining oil, allow to heat, then add the potatoes and cook for a further 15-20 minutes, until they are tender. Season with salt and drain off any excess oil.

3 Mix the vinegar and garlic together, pour over the potatoes and then stir. Serve immediately

'Most of our recipes are traditional and hardly vary,' says Raquel. 'The only one we won't reveal is the Chupi chupi. *That's basically a superior open sandwich of good country bread made with beef and a special sauce. My father tasted it in Barcelona, developed the recipe and it became the house speciality.'*

ANDALUCIA

Manuel Zamora
Casablanca

Rosa María Bórja
Isabel Capote Dominguez
La Eslava

Lola Gracía Burgos
Emiliano Sánchez Pincón
Bar Giralda

Julián González Carasco
Juan Gutierrez Moreno
Bodegas Campos

Lourdes Ybarra
Bar Europa

Enrique Becerra
Diego Ruíz
Enrique Becer...

No region embodies Moorish Spain as clearly as Andalucía. Other parts of the peninsula may harbour the odd discernible trace of the Moors, but it is in the great arid swathe of the south that the 800-year-old Moorish occupation really made an unrivalled impact. Architecture, crafts, music, agriculture, fiery eyes and fiery cuisine are the obvious legacies of a culture that ended in 1492, when the Spanish Catholics captured the Moors' most extraordinary creation: the Alhambra palace, queen of Granada. Looking back at his conquered kingdom, the boy-king Boabdil shed a tear, breathed his 'last

temperatures never descend far and rainfall is rare, even in the winter months, making the problem of drought increasingly urgent.

This issue was something the Moors understood when they set about irrigating huge tracts of land to cultivate a wealth of produce that was previously unknown to the Iberians. This cultivation is what led to many Spanish food words beginning with the typically Arabic syllable 'al' (as in *alcachofa*, artichoke; *alazán*, sorrel; *albahaca*, basil; and *almíbar*, syrup).

Not only this, but the Moorish occupiers also added layers to the

'...olive trees march over the horizon, almond trees explode into frothy pink and white blossom, fighting bulls graze in the Guadalquivír valley, oranges dangle from town-centre foliage, goats trip up rocky hillsides, whitebait and tuna are netted off Cádiz...'

sigh' and fled into exile. The mountain pass he followed still bears this epithet, as does so much else in Andalucía that is connected to the Moors. If you have a 'last tapa' – make it here.

Lunar landscapes of karst and shale roll into the heat-haze, olive trees march over the horizon, almond trees explode into frothy pink and white blossom, fighting bulls graze in the Guadalquivír valley, oranges dangle from town-centre foliage, goats trip up rocky hillsides, whitebait and tuna are netted off Cádiz and, in the south-east, vast fields of *plásticas* (plastic greenhouses) force-grow much of Europe's supply of the best avocados, artichokes, tomatoes and green beans on an all-year-round basis. The region's

previous Roman and Iberian tastes with their vast orange and lemon groves, chilled vegetable soup (*gazpacho*), dates and sugar-cane. The sweet tooth hit town, and it is still evident in the many dishes and sweets that include honey or dried fruits. It is said tapas originated in Seville and, whether this is true or not, the city's inhabitants are certainly masters of the art.

Hedonistic, rococo, extrovert, Seville possesses little of Córdoba's poetic gravitas that filters through the arches of the Mezquita, or Granada's noble setting. Seville is a composite of stage sets, each one a tiny *plaza* more often than not flanked by a saffron-coloured church, orange trees and a couple of tapas bars for easy exits to the wings.

The *sevilliano's* sense of drama peaks during *Semana Santa* (Easter week) and *Feria* (April fair), when the women strut in the flounces of their flamenco dresses or in their sharp riding-suits and gaucho hats, while the men in penitents' hoods heave statues of Christ or, clad in riding gear, direct their mounts with macho panache to the nearest source of *fino*.

Throughout the year, popular tapas bars in Seville see people spilling out on to the pavement or squeezing up on a corner ledge or a sherry-barrel in order to wolf down their ever-varied tapas lunch. You could virtually set your watch by these social gatherings.

The classic Sevillian tipple comes from nearby Jerez de la Frontera. The origins of sherry have their roots, as do all Spanish wines, with the Phoenicians, but sherry, a fortified wine, was developed over the centuries as a way of avoiding spoilage. It became popular in England during the 16th century, after Sir Francis Drake seized nearly 3,000 barrels of it from the Spanish Armada in 1587. Well-to-do Londoners in particular developed a taste for the stolen wine, and this was the genesis of a flourishing industry that left English merchants' names attached to numerous *bodegas* or wineries.

From the refreshing, tongue-searingly dry *fino*, to the honey-coloured *amontillado*, rich golden *oloroso* and finally the syrupy *dulce*, sherry's incarnations suit every palate and tapa – despite the local preference for *manzanilla*, a somewhat saltier version of *fino* that is produced in the seaside town of Sanlúcar de Barrameda. When not consuming their sherry chilled, Andalucians use it in vinegar form as a piquant addition to gazpachos and vegetable-based tapas.

Bull-fighting plays a fanatical role in Andalucía's multiple *fiestas*, making *rabo de toro* (oxtail) an entrenched favourite on the region's tapas menu, though the recent threat of bovine diseases has put the brakes on this particular taste. Fresh seafood is a permanent feature on the menus too, whether in the umpteen tapas bars found along the coast or in the heart of inland Andalucía.

Stand on a bridge crossing the Guadalquivír river in Seville, 90km (56 miles) from the estuary, and you can sniff the salt in the air, as did Ferdinand Magellan, Juan Sebastián Elcano and Christopher Columbus, all of whom set sail from here during Spain's big push across the high seas. Latin American plunder brought back in their ships' holds financed the city's wealth of monuments, peaking in the 17th century baroque and reflected in the great Sevillian school of painting by Pacheco, Velázquez and Murillo.

Other New World booty took the more prosaic form of potatoes, tomatoes, corn, cocoa, haricot beans – and, of course, tobacco. Seville's old tobacco factory, which is situated right next to the riverine harbour, contains the shadow of the legendary Carmen stamping her feet and howling for love. That pungent whiff of Ducados permeates many a tapas bar, while the food imported from the Americas produced yet another sea change in Andalucian cuisine.

It's hard not to feel it: Andalucía is about passion and tragedy, about emotions, extremes, strong flavours, hot sun and cool soups. Cook the tapas of this magnetic region and you'll be propelled into an extraordinary world – and make sure the volume of the flamenco music is turned up high!

Manuel Zamora   Casablanca, Seville

Casablanca is another of Andalucía's hidden secrets, tucked down a side-street in central Seville behind a nondescript closed door. Push it open and you enter a tiny gastronomic heaven frequented by Seville's top brass and the odd bullfighter. The chef, a generous, ebullient Andaluz in his early 40s, Manuel Zamora, thinks, breathes – and probably dreams – food. 'I started as a dishwasher in a five-star restaurant at the age of 15 and never stopped asking the cooks and staff questions about what was being made,' he says. He kept this questioning attitude as he worked his way up the ladder, via Las Palmas, to the Parador de Carmona, before entering the highly-rated Casablanca. Today, having cooked tapas, lunches and dinners for six days of the week, Manuel will spend his day off tending the olive trees, tomatoes and doves in his vegetable garden or looking at cookery books.

Intuitive in his approach, Manuel is also sensitive to his customers' tastes. 'I'm inspired by what I see in the market and 90 per cent of what I use is Andalucian. Even the foie gras is local and the demi-glace is typically Spanish. There's no menu here and every dish we make must be excellent.' The one tapa fixture is Seasoned potato mash, served with your first drink (free, as in tradition) and much imitated but never equalled by other tapas bars.

Seasoned potato mash
Patatas aliñadas

for 6 tapas
*1k (2¹/₄lb) new potatoes, scrubbed
3 spring onions, white part only,
finely chopped
3 green peppers, finely chopped
9 tbsp extra virgin olive oil, preferably
from a single estate
3 tbsp white wine vinegar
salt and pepper*

Casablanca's hallmark tapa of seasoned mash is generously bathed in virgin olive oil from Baena – rated as Andalucía's premier oil. Don't worry if you can't get hold of this oil, but do use the best you can find. Typically for Manuel, this is a delicious tapa created from the simplest ingredients.

1 Cook the potatoes in boiling salted water for about 20 minutes, or until they are tender.

2 Remove the skins and mash the potatoes, then push the mash through a sieve or potato ricer. Add the finely chopped onions and peppers.

3 Slowly add the oil and vinegar, beating until the mash is thick and creamy. (If more is necessary, add in proportions of 3 oil to 1 vinegar.)

4 Season with salt and pepper and serve immediately, mounded on to small individual plates.

Seafood pasta
Fideos a la marinera

for 6 tapas

1 medium onion, diced

2 medium green peppers, diced

2 tomatoes, diced

2 cloves garlic, minced

olive oil for frying

75ml (2^1/$_2$fl oz) white wine

1 litre (1^3/$_4$ pints) water

^{1}/$_4$ tsp saffron threads, infused in just a little boiled water

250g (9oz) clams, scrubbed and washed and any that will not close discarded

150g (5^1/$_2$oz) cuttlefish, cleaned, prepared and cut into small strips

150g (5^1/$_2$oz) prawns, peeled

100g (3^1/$_2$oz) hake, filleted and cut into small pieces

salt and pepper to taste

200g (7oz) short lengths of spaghetti or a pasta shape such as tubetti lunghi

Although fiddly to prepare, this tapa looks and tastes stunning and you may want to increase the quantities to make it into a main dish.

1 In a heavy-bottomed sauté pan, fry the onion, peppers, tomatoes and garlic in olive oil until soft.

2 Add the white wine and cook for about 10 minutes to reduce the liquid.

3 Add the water and saffron liquid and cook on a high heat for 15 minutes.

4 Add the clams, cuttlefish, prawns, hake, seasoning and pasta and continue to cook over a low heat for about 10 minutes, until the fish and pasta are tender and the liquid has been absorbed. Discard any clams that have not opened. Serve in individual earthenware dishes.

Potato tortilla
Tortilla de patatas

for 6 tapas
100ml (3¹/2fl oz) olive oil
1k (2¹/4lb) potatoes, peeled and cubed
3 eggs, beaten
salt and pepper to taste

Manuel serves this classic Spanish *tortilla*, typically made with potatoes, with an ambrosial sauce based on whisky (see below).

1 Heat the olive oil in a frying pan. Cook the potatoes in the oil over a very low heat for about 15 minutes, until they are tender but not brown.

2 In a bowl, mix the potatoes with the beaten eggs and season to taste. Pour the mixture back into the frying pan and cook over a low heat for 3-4 minutes. When the *tortilla* is firm but not dry, cover the frying pan with a plate of equal size and, grasping the plate and pan, turn the *tortilla* out on to the plate.

3 Carefully slide the *tortilla* back into the pan and cook for another 3 minutes to brown the other side.

4 Turn out on to a serving plate and cool for at least 5 minutes. Slices can be served hot or at room temperature, covered with whisky sauce (see below).

'I'm inspired by what I see in the market and 90 per cent of what I use is Andalucian. Even the foie gras is local and the demi-glace I use is typically Spanish.'

Whisky sauce
Salsa de whisky

for 6 tapas
3 cloves garlic, finely sliced
2 tbsp olive oil
15g (¹/2oz) butter
1 tbsp lemon juice
1 tbsp whisky
1 tbsp strong beef stock

Manuel serves this sauce as an accompaniment for the above *tortilla* - a combination that may sound odd but, given the Andalucian enthusiasm for high spirits, it is hardly surprising! This sauce also tastes good with meats such as beef.

1 Sauté the garlic slices in the olive oil until they are tender.

2 Add the butter, lemon juice, whisky and beef stock. Cook over a low heat, stirring occasionally, for 15 minutes, until reduced.

Chicken legs with prunes and nuts in a blackberry sauce
Pularda rellena de frutos secos en salsa de zarzamora

for 12 tapas

75g (2³/₄oz) pine nuts
50g (1³/₄oz) walnuts, shelled and chopped
50g (1³/₄oz) unsalted pistachios, shelled and chopped
125g (4¹/₂oz) pitted prunes, chopped
12 organic chicken legs, boned
salt and pepper to taste
2 tbsp olive oil
200g (7oz) cloves garlic
2 small onions, sliced into half moons
2 potatoes, in 3mm (¹/₂ inch) slices
250ml (9fl oz) sweet Málaga wine

for the blackberry sauce

125g (4¹/₄oz) fresh or frozen blackberries
100g (3¹/₂oz) granulated sugar
2 tbsp balsamic vinegar

Moorish influences rule in this luscious concoction of prunes, nuts, fresh fruit, chicken and sweet wine. Note that any dark dessert wine can be substituted for the Málaga variety.

1 Mix the nuts and prunes together, then stuff the chicken legs with the mixture. Tie each leg together with kitchen string.

2 Place the stuffed legs on baking sheets, season, drizzle with olive oil, surround with garlic cloves, onions and potatoes, and bake in an oven preheated to 200ºC (400º F) Gas mark 6 for 30-35 minutes, until the chicken is cooked.

3 Make the sauce by heating the berries and sugar with a few tbsp water, stirring to help the sugar dissolve in the berry juices. Add the vinegar, bring to the boil, then cook until syrupy – remember, it will thicken more as it cools. Set aside.

4 Warm the wine. Transfer the chicken legs, garlic and onions to a platter, pour the warmed wine over them and flambé immediately by touching the edge of the platter with the flame of a match. Serve the chicken accompanied by the sauce.

Andalucian-style spinach with chickpeas
Espinacas con garbanzos a la andaluza

for 6 tapas

1k (2lb 4oz) fresh spinach, washed, and destalked
50ml (2fl oz) olive oil
300g (10¹/₂oz) cooked chickpeas, drained
1 tsp ground cumin
salt and pepper to taste
3 cloves garlic
1 slice bread, fried in oil until golden
1 tsp red wine vinegar
2 tbsp water
1¹/₂ tsp sweet paprika

This classic Andalucian dish has travelled to tapas bars all over Spain, such is its earthy appeal. The spinach and chickpeas are, surprisingly, Moorish imports.

1 Cook the spinach in a covered pan, in the water that clings to it after washing, for about 4 minutes, until it is wilted. Let it cool, then press out the excess water. Chop roughly.

2 Sauté the spinach in the oil on a low heat for about a minute. Stir in the chickpeas, cumin, salt and pepper.

3 Pound the garlic and fried bread with a pestle and mortar or grind them in a blender until fine. Add to the spinach and mix well.

4 Add the vinegar, water and paprika, and cook over a low heat, stirring constantly, for about a minute. Serve at once in individual earthenware dishes.

Rosa María Bórja
Isabel Capote Dominguez   La Eslava, Seville

You could easily miss out on La Eslava, for it is tucked down a back street off the vast Alameda de Hércules. Yet this hip haunt is quintessentially Sevillian, netting an eclectic range of customers, from local artists and intellectuals to those in the know from further afield. Behind the bar the energetic owner, Sixto Tovar Gutierrez, juggles phone-calls with tapas or beers, while in the kitchen his French wife, Rosa María Bórja, accomplishes La Eslava's miracles in tandem with Isabel Capote Dominguez.

According to Isabel, 'Together with vegetables, olive oil is the most important characteristic of Andalucian cuisine.' Describing the approach of this glamorous duet to cooking, she says 'When we make a new dish, we look at the colours and flavours, but if it doesn't taste right we abandon it.' Rosa María appreciates suggestions from her customers. 'Our customers propose ideas which we follow up. They adore soups,' she says, 'as they take a long time to prepare at home.' Ask her to compare Andalucía with her native South-West France and Rosa María cheerfully admits 'French food is of course very good, but Andalucía's basic produce has far more flavour. The gazpacho my mother made in Toulouse was never as good as the gazpacho they make here.' Even better is La Eslava's renowned salmorejo, to be imitated but never surpassed.

Spinach prawn loaf
Pudin de espinacas

for 4 tapas
*400g (14oz) spinach, washed
and destalked
1 medium onion, finely chopped
2 medium tomatoes, finely chopped
2 tbsp olive oil
100g (3 1/2 oz) raw prawns, peeled
salt and pepper to taste
125ml (4fl oz) milk
125ml (4fl oz) double cream
4 eggs*

This cold, mousse-like tapa is ideal for hot weather, when appetites are not too big. La Eslava's customers favour beer or sangría as their summer drinks, and this tapa makes the perfect accompaniment for either.

1 Cook the spinach in the water that clings to the leaves after washing, in a covered saucepan over a medium heat for about 4 minutes. Drain and wring the excess water out by pressing the cooked leaves between two dinner plates - the spinach must be very dry. Set aside.

2 Sauté the onion and tomatoes in the olive oil until tender. Turn the heat up to make some of the liquid evaporates. Add the spinach and prawns, season and stir. Cook over a low heat for a few minutes, then cool.

3 Put the prawn and spinach mixture into a blender and add the milk, cream and eggs. Whirl until smooth and creamy. Taste for seasoning.

4 Pour the mixture into a lightly oiled loaf tin and bake in a bain-marie at 180ºC (350ºF) Gas mark 4 for about 45 minutes, until firm. To test if the loaf is cooked, insert a skewer into the centre - it should come out clean. Cool, then refrigerate for at least 2 hours.

5 To serve, unmould and cut into slices of desired thickness.

Chilled tomato garlic soup
Salmorejo

for 4 tapas
500g (1lb 2oz) ripe tomatoes
*225g (8oz) day-old bread, torn
into pieces*
250ml (9fl oz) olive oil
1 tbsp sherry vinegar
1 clove garlic
salt and pepper to taste
*55g (2oz) serrano ham,
chopped (optional)*
1 hard-boiled egg, chopped (optional)

Although *salmorejo* originated in Córdoba, neighbouring Seville has taken to it with passion. It is basically a thicker, creamier version of gazpacho, and it works equally well as a soup or dip. The most important element, the tomatoes, must be plump and juicy or the soup will lack its *raison d'être*.

1 Combine the tomatoes and bread in a blender and mix well. Add the oil, vinegar, garlic, salt and pepper and blend until smooth and thick.

2 Serve as a dip with chunks of French bread or as a soup, drizzled with extra virgin olive oil. You may add a sprinkling of diced serrano ham and chopped hard-boiled egg if desired.

Potato and cod stew
Purrusalda

for 4 tapas
250g (9oz) salt cod
4 leeks, cleaned and coarsely chopped
4 tbsp olive oil
1kg (2¹/4lb) potatoes, peeled and diced
1¹/4 litres (1³/4 pints) fish stock
3 ripe tomatoes, chopped
salt and pepper to taste

The classic marriage of cod and potatoes has been developed by Rosa María and Isabel into a hearty, appetising tapa, lifted by Mediterranean tomatoes and olive oil.

1 Soak the salt cod in water for 2 days, changing the water a couple of times a day. Rinse. Flake the flesh, leaving any bones and the skin behind.

2 In a large pan, sauté the leeks in the olive oil until tender. Add the potatoes and continue to sauté over a very low heat for 15 more minutes.

3 Add the fish stock and tomatoes, bring to the boil, and simmer for 20 minutes.

4 Add the flaked salt cod and simmer for 10 more minutes. Season to taste, and serve hot in individual soup bowls.

'Together with vegetables, olive oil is the most important characteristic of Andalucian cuisine.'

Honey-baked chicken thighs
Muslos de pollo a la miel

for 4 tapas
250g (9oz) liquid honey
100g (3¹/2oz) butter
1 tsp curry powder
1¹/2 tsp dry mustard powder
75ml (2¹/2fl oz) tomato ketchup
8 chicken thighs

This simple recipe offers some interesting flavour contrasts, all dominated by the sweetness of the honey – yet another Moorish legacy. It makes an excellent tapa to accompany dry white wine or dry sherry on a summer's day.

1 To prepare the honey sauce, combine all the ingredients except for the chicken thighs in a saucepan. Mix well and bring to a boil. Remove from the heat.

2 Place the chicken thighs in a roasting tin, pour over the sauce, and bake in a pre-heated oven at 180°C (350°F) Gas mark 4 for about 35 minutes, or until the chicken is dark and glossy and cooked through. Serve immediately.

Lola Gracía Burgos
Emiliano Sánchez Pincón   Bar Giralda, Seville

Just behind Seville's emblematic Giralda - a towering 12th century minaret topped by a Renaissance belfry - lies a bar with the self-same name, converted in 1934 from Arab baths into one of Seville's most architecturally stunning watering-holes. Run by Francisco Sánchez González, its zelij-tiled walls, vaulted ceilings, stuccoed arches and marble-topped tables create a classic meeting-place for Sevillian society. As it is open from breakfast through to the early hours, Bar Giralda functions more like a Parisian grand café than a traditional tapas bar.

Sevillians gather here not only for the elegant setting, but also for the constantly changing tapas menu. This is the work of Francisco's wife, Lola Gracía Burgos, and the chef, Emiliano Sánchez Pincón, a sevilliano by birth who has perfected his art in Bar Giralda's kitchen over the last 19 years.

'I started working here when I was 17 and learnt everything I know from the other cooks,' he says. 'The tapas are now a collaboration between Lola and myself. We're always experimenting and varying the list.' On the blackboard is scrawled the tapa of the day, generally based on meat or fish, as well as the rest of the tapas menu. 'Seville represents the heart of Andalucian traditions, so we try to reflect that,' continues Emiliano. 'Malaga, for example, concentrates mainly on seafood. But the ingredients that are eternal are onions, tomatoes and red peppers - I couldn't do without them.' And few sevillianos could do without this retreat.

Potatoes of great importance
Patatas a la importancia

for 4 tapas

2 large potatoes, peeled and cut in 1cm (¹/2-inch) slices
100g (3¹/2oz) cooked ham, in thin slices
100g (3¹/2oz) French Chaumes or Port Salut cheese, in thin slices
salt to taste
beaten egg for coating
flour for coating
250ml (9fl oz) olive oil for frying

for the sauce

2 tbsp olive oil
7 cloves garlic, thinly sliced
1 bunch flat-leaf parsley, chopped
2 tbsp flour
250ml (9fl oz) white wine

This is another of Spain's sustaining 'peasant' snacks, made from basic ingredients with strong flavours.

1 Between each 2 potato slices, place 1 slice of ham and 1 slice of cheese. Season with salt. Dip in beaten egg, then flour, and fry in hot oil until the potato is golden and cooked. Remove.

2 To make the sauce, heat the oil in a frying pan. Add the garlic and sauté until tender. Add the parsley and stir. Blend in the flour, stirring until the mixture has thickened. Take the pan off the heat and stir constantly while adding the wine a little at a time.

3 When the wine is incorporated, put the pan back on the heat and bring to the boil, stirring. Simmer for 5 minutes. Pour the sauce over the potatoes and serve immediately.

Roast chicken breasts stuffed with salmon
Pechugas de pollo rellenas de salmón con salsa de curry

for 4 tapas
2 chicken breast fillets
olive oil
150g (5¹/₂oz) sliced smoked salmon
pepper to taste
curry sauce (see below)

This simple but effective tapa can be prepared in advance and heated at the last minute. Organic chicken is best as it tends to be more flavoursome, standing up to the strong flavours of the salmon and curry sauce.

1 Place the chicken breasts on a rack in a shallow pan and brush with olive oil. Season and roast in an oven preheated to 150°C (300°F) Gas mark 2 for about 25 minutes. The chicken should be almost cooked – check by cutting into the breast with a sharp knife. Cool slightly. Reduce the oven to 120°C (250°F) Gas mark 1.

2 Slice each breast in half lengthways, without cutting completely through, and open. Stuff with several slices of salmon and season with pepper. Wrap in aluminium foil and place in a shallow baking tray. Return to the oven for 20 minutes, or until the chicken is cooked through.

3 Remove the chicken from the foil. Cut each breast crosswise into 4 slices, arrange these on a platter and pour the curry sauce over the top. Serve the tapa immediately.

Curry sauce
Salsa de curry

for 4 tapas
¹/₂ large onion
1 tsp curry powder
125ml (4fl oz) mayonnaise

This sauce is ideal with the salmon-stuffed chicken breasts (above), or served with bread as a spicy dip.

1 Remove the outer layer of the onion. Parboil the rest of the onion, drain, cool and finely chop.

2 Combine all the ingredients in a blender and mix well.

Julián González Carasco
Juan Gutierrez Moreno   Bodegas Campos, Córdoba

The sober frontage of Córdoba's most successful restaurant spells out its attitude to food: quality and finesse. This is what attracts the town's movers and shakers to dine here in studied calm. Between the rooms of this labyrinthine restaurant lie typically Cordoban patios – thick with perfumes and bright with geraniums – shady corridors lined with sherry barrels and tiled floors clicking with the heels of fame. More than anywhere else, Bodegas Campos encapsulates a journey into the heart of Andalucía. Since it opened in 1908, the restaurant has fed a stream of celebrities, from the Duchess of Alba to Joaquin Cortés, Paco Peña and Tony Blair. But despite its success, Bodegas Campos maintains a personal approach. Keeping appetites satisfied are four chefs and 20 cooks, headed by Julián González Carasco and Juan Gutierrez Moreno. For Juan, 'Andalucian cuisine is the best - after French, which is the basis of everything. Our advantage lies in the quality of our products: the fresh fish and vegetables and the excellent oils and vinegars.' The old mantra 'quality, quality, quality' is behind the exquisite tapas which, although simple to prepare, keep rulers, matadors and divas hooked.

Chilled tomato soup with aged sherry vinegar
Gazpacho de tomate con vinagre de Pedro Ximénez

for 4 tapas
1kg (2¹/₄lb) plump, vine-ripened tomatoes, chopped
500g (1lb 2oz) fresh breadcrumbs made from a crusty loaf
175ml (6fl oz) Pedro Ximénez vinegar or similar mature, sherry vinegar
500ml (18fl oz) extra virgin olive oil
salt and pepper to taste

This is one of many *gazpacho* recipes, a more liquid soup than *salmorejo*, but similarly dependent on juicy, flavoursome tomatoes. A dish with this much sherry vinegar is something of an acquired taste, so start by adding a quarter of the quantity given and add the rest to taste. This *gazpacho* can be served with little side-dishes of diced ham, green pepper, cucumber and tomatoes to sprinkle on top. More like a superior, seasoned tomato juice, it makes the ultimate refreshing summer tapa.

1 Put all the ingredients into a blender and then blend to a smooth, thick but juicy consistency.

2 Taste and adjust the seasoning. Refrigerate for at least 2 hours. Serve cold in glasses with a drizzle of olive oil.

Country-style potatoes with chorizo and peppers
Patatas cortijeras con picadillo de chorizo

for 4 tapas

*400g (14oz) potatoes, peeled and
thinly sliced*

50g (1³/4oz) unsalted butter

3 tbsp olive oil for frying

125g (4¹/2oz) onion, thinly sliced

20g (³/4oz) red pepper, thinly sliced

20g (³/4oz) green pepper, thinly sliced

3 cloves garlic, thinly sliced

*30g (1oz) serrano ham, cut into
thin strips*

*50g (1³/4oz) chorizo, cut into 1cm
(¹/2-inch) slices and lightly fried*

2 eggs

salt and pepper to taste

Developed in the kitchen by Julián and Juan, this recipe exploits the abundant fresh local vegetables, with the chorizo and ham acting as little more than seasoning. It's a perfect, sustaining *mélange* enveloped by lightly-cooked egg.

1 Fry the potatoes in the butter and 2 tbsp of the oil over a low heat for 25 minutes, until the potatoes are tender. Remove the potatoes, leaving the fat behind, and put them in a bowl. Set aside.

2 In the same frying pan, sauté the onion and peppers over a low heat, adding more oil if you need it. When the vegetables are tender, add the garlic and cook until it is golden.

3 Add the vegetable mixture to the potatoes, stir in the meats and set aside.

4 Fry the eggs in a little oil until the white is firm. Add them to the vegetable and meat mixture and stir to break the eggs up. Combine all the ingredients. Season and tip on to a serving platter.

Fried pork loin and ham balls
Bolitas de flamenquín

for 6 tapas

250g (9oz) pork loin, cut into thin slices lengthways
juice of 1 lemon
100g (3¹/₂oz) Iberian or serrano ham, cut into 6 slices
salt and pepper to taste
25g (1oz) flour
2 eggs, beaten
55g (2oz) dry breadcrumbs
olive oil for frying

Quite simply delicious, this is an excellent tapa for large numbers of people, as the meatballs can be prepared in advance and served cold. The zing of the lemon juice makes all the difference.

1 Marinate the pork loin in the lemon juice for 1 hour.

2 Place a piece of ham on each pork slice, season, and roll up lengthwise to form cylinders.

3 Cut each cylinder into 2cm (³/₄-inch) pieces, and squeeze into ball shapes.

4 Dip the balls in flour, then egg, then breadcrumbs and fry a few at a time in very hot oil, browning on all sides. Drain on paper towels and serve promptly.

'Andalucian cuisine is the best – after French, which is the basis of everything. Our advantage lies in the quality of our products: the fresh fish and vegetables and the excellent oils and vinegars.'

Frittata of garden vegetables
Fritura de la huerta

for 4 tapas

40g (1¹/₂oz) onion, cut into thin rings
25g (1oz) flour
55g (2oz) cauliflower, separated into florets and briefly cooked
1 egg, beaten
55g (2oz) dry breadcrumbs
55g (2oz) aubergine, peeled and cut into small cubes
1 tbsp milk
olive oil for frying
salt to taste

The choice of vegetables is yours but, as always, follow the seasons for the best results; obvious alternatives to those in this recipe are green and red peppers. The light batter produces a crisp coating that resembles tempura.

1 Dip the onion rings in flour. Dip the cauliflower first in flour, then in egg, then in breadcrumbs. Moisten the aubergine cubes in milk and then coat with flour.

2 Heat about 6cm (2¹/₂ inches) olive oil in a pan and, when hot, cook the vegetables seperately. Drain immediately on paper towels and then sprinkle with salt.

3 Arrange attractively on a plate and serve promptly with a *salmorejo* dip (see page 168).

Lourdes Ybarra   Bar Europa, Seville

In the last year of the 20th century, Bar Europa underwent a major facelift under the guidance of its new owner, Neus Bragat from Barcelona. Before her aegis, this was a neglected, family-owned bar whose cuisine was limited to tripe stew. By restoring the premises to its original 1920s splendour, Neus put this classic Sevillian tapas bar back on the map and at the same time injected northern elements into the menu. It is now one of the few places in Seville to serve cava, and the changing tapas menu sometimes features white or black butifarra (black pudding) or similar Catalan specialities. The menu aside, though, Bar Europa embodies a typically elegant Sevillian setting.

Easily visible through the kitchen hatch behind the long, wooden bar is the chef, Lourdes Ybarra, a native of a nearby village, where she ran her own bar before coming to the big city. 'Most of my ideas and methods come either from cooking school or from my grandmother,' she says. 'I had seven brothers and sisters and, although I was the youngest, I ended up doing all the cooking. It's simply something I love doing!' Something to bear in mind when preparing any of her tapas.

Chilled almond soup
Ajo blanco

for 4 tapas

250g (9oz) blanched almonds
3 cloves garlic
85g (3oz) white breadcrumbs
500ml (18fl oz) water
2 tbsp sherry vinegar
salt to taste
6 tbsp olive oil
8 Muscatel (or similar) grapes
extra virgin olive oil to serve

This soup, invented by the Moors to counteract Andalucía's baking hot summers, can look divinely minimalist served in white bowls afloat with white muscatel grapes. It makes a refreshing change from some of Andalucía's stronger flavours, as the almond is extremely subtle.

1 Finely grind the almonds and garlic in a blender. Add the breadcrumbs, water, vinegar and salt and blend for 2 minutes until smooth.

2 Slowly add the olive oil, while continuing to blend, until you have a creamy liquid. Refrigerate for at least 1 hour.

3 Serve in individual soup bowls, with a grape or two and a light drizzle of extra virgin olive oil in each one.

Salt cod and orange salad
Ensalada de bacalao con naranja

for 4 tapas
800g (1³/4lb) salt cod
300g (10¹/2oz) juicy orange segments,
skin and pips removed, diced
2 tbsp snipped chives
4 black olives
extra virgin olive oil to taste

This ultra-simple tapa offers a refreshing combination of flavours, but it is essential to use good quality salt cod and luscious oranges. If you have individual moulds, so much the better, as cutting slices of this salad tends to make it crumble.

1 Soak the salt cod in water for 48 hours, changing the water a couple of times a day. Remove the flesh, discard the skin and bones, and flake the flesh.

2 Mix the orange flesh with the chives, then divide the mixture into individual moulds. Top with the flaked salt cod and compress well.

3 Refrigerate for at least 1 hour before turning upside-down on to plates to serve.

4 Decorate each portion with a black olive and drizzle with olive oil.

Ratatouille with quail's egg
Pisto con huevo de codorniz

for 4 tapas
6 green peppers, diced
1 large onion, diced
olive oil
500g (1lb 2oz) aubergine, peeled
and diced
500g (1lb 2oz) courgette, diced
500g (1lb 2oz) tomatoes, diced
salt and pepper to taste
4 quail's eggs

Pisto originated in La Mancha, but soon conquered the south and became Andalucía's answer to Provençal ratatouille - a mixture of braised Mediterranean vegetables - served with a fried egg. When preparing the vegetables, keep them in separate dishes so that you can easily add them successively.

1 In a large pan, sauté the peppers and onion in about 2 tbsp olive oil until they are tender. Add the aubergine and sauté for 5 more minutes. Add the courgette and sauté for 3 more minutes. You may need more oil.

2 Add the tomatoes, lower the heat, and simmer the vegetables together for 20 minutes. Season 5 minutes before the cooking time has ended.

3 Quickly fry the quail's eggs in a little olive oil.

4 To serve, heap generous portions of ratatouille on to individual serving plates and top with a fried egg.

Enrique Becerra
Diego Ruiz   Enrique Becerra, Seville

This humming tapas bar, within one of Seville's most successful restaurants, was opened in 1979 by Enrique Becerra, a Sevillian with five generations of bar-restaurants pumping through his blood. The tapas menu changes daily, the result of a collaboration between Enrique and his head chef, Diego Ruiz. Madrid-born and trained, Diego started working in restaurants at the age of 15, remaining in the capital until he took over the ovens at Enrique Becerra three years ago. 'The basic produce here – such as vegetables, chickpeas, lentils and chorizo – is excellent,' he says. 'In the north they go for more sophisticated foods such as baby eel, caviar or smoked salmon, but you can do fantastic things with simple, good-quality ingredients.'

Diego is lucid about his profession, too: 'It requires long hours and total dedication, but cooking is about inspiration – like any art form. The main thing is to like what you're doing,' he says. So perch on a bar-stool, order a Manzanilla, pick at Becerra's succulent olives, and you'll soon be humming a few bars from Carmen.

Asparagus and prawn flans
Pudin de espárragos verdes y gambas

for 4 tapas

¹/₂ medium onion, finely chopped
olive oil
100g (3¹/₂oz) prawns, peeled and chopped
100g (3¹/₂oz) green asparagus, preferably wild, cut into small pieces
50ml (2fl oz) dry sherry
225ml (8fl oz) whipping cream
3 eggs, beaten
salt and white pepper to taste
mayonnaise to serve

The Spanish word *'pudin'*, an aborted version of the English 'pudding', is used to describe a savoury tapa that resembles a French mousse. This version has a pleasingly rough texture and undemanding flavours.

1 A day before serving, sauté the onion in a little olive oil until it is soft.

2 Add the prawns, asparagus and sherry and cook over a low heat until the liquid has almost disappeared.

3 Add the whipping cream, beaten eggs and a little salt and pepper and mix well.

4 Pour into lightly oiled individual daniole moulds. Set these in a bain-marie and bake in an oven pre-heated to 180ºC (350ºF) Gas mark 4 for 35 minutes. Remove from the oven, cool and then refrigerate for 12 hours.

5 Just before serving, turn the flans out, place on individual plates, and top each one with a dollop of mayonnaise.

Lentil and chorizo stew
Lentejas estofadas

for 4 tapas
225g (8oz) green or brown lentils,
soaked overnight
75ml (2¹/₂fl oz) virgin olive oil
1¹/₂ tsp Spanish paprika
1 small green pepper, diced
1 small onion, peeled and diced
1 small ripe tomato, peeled and diced
1 bay leaf
3 cloves garlic
100g (3¹/₂oz) chorizo or other spicy
sausage, sliced
100g (3¹/₂oz) black pudding, sliced
1 small carrot, peeled and sliced
200g (7oz) potatoes, peeled and diced

Well-blended, earthy flavours are the characteristics of this classic tapa, simply prepared according to Diego's tastes.

1 Combine all the ingredients, except for the potatoes, in a heavy saucepan. Cover with cold water and bring to the boil. Reduce the heat and simmer for about 20 minutes.

2 Add the potatoes and continue to simmer for about 20 more minutes, until the potatoes and lentils are tender. Serve hot in individual earthenware dishes.

Minted lamb meatballs
Albóndigas de cordero a la hierbabuena

for 6 tapas
500g (1lb 2oz) lamb, minced
salt and pepper to taste
3 cloves garlic, minced
3 tbsp chopped fresh mint
2 small eggs, beaten
4 tbsp soft breadcrumbs
100ml (3¹/₂fl oz) dry sherry
1 tbsp olive oil for sautéing

For the sauce
2 onions, finely chopped
1 clove garlic, finely chopped
1 tbsp olive oil for sautéing
225ml (8fl oz) thick tomato passata
1 tbsp dry sherry
water to thin, if needed

Although Spain offers numerous variants on the meatball theme, these are arguably the tastiest!

1 Combine all the meatball ingredients except for the olive oil in a large bowl and mix well. Form the meat into 2.5cm (1-inch) diameter balls and sauté in oil until lightly browned on all sides. Drain on paper towels and set aside.

2 In the same pan, sauté the onions and garlic for the sauce in olive oil until soft. Add the tomato passata and sherry and simmer for 10 minutes. Remove from the heat.

3 In a blender, purée the sauce until smooth, adding a little water if it's too thick. Return the sauce to the sauté pan and add the meatballs. Bring to the boil and cook over a medium heat for about 10 minutes. Serve hot.

RECOMMENDED TAPAS BARS

* bars featured in this book

BASQUE REGION

Aloña Berri Bar, Calle Bermingham 24, Gros, San Sebastián Tel: 943 290818
A mouthful of hot foie gras with fig or a tasty bite of crab or langoustine are among the offerings at one of San Sebastián's most sophisticated tapas bars.

Casa Bartolo, Calle Fermín Calbetón 38, San Sebastián Tel: 943 421743
Mean classics of Basque cuisine are served in tapas portions at the bar. Bacalao pil pil (Salt cod cooked with olive oil and garlic), Bacalao a la vizcaina (Salt cod in a tomato, onion and pepper sauce) and Bacalao encebollado (Salt cod with onions) are the stars.

*Baserri, Calle San Nicolas, 32, 31001 Pamplona Tel: 948 222021
www.restaurantebaserri.com
In a street that is wall-to-wall tapas bars with a bacalao shop thrown in for good measure, this is the ultimate destination for top-class food.

*Bar Bergara, Calle General Artetxe 8, Gros, San Sebastián Tel: 943 275026
Pintxos faithfuls flock to this prize-winning temple of delicacies in San Sebastián's art deco quarter. Whether warm or cold, each dish is a work of art.

*La Cuchara de San Telmo, Calle 31 de Agosto 28, San Sebastián Tel: 943 420840
Revel in imaginative concoctions of miniature gourmet cuisine if you can squeeze your way into the bar. Outside on the terrace, relax in the shadow of the old church of San Telmo.

Bar Fitero, Calle Estafeta 58, Pamplona Tel: 948 222006
A third generation works hard to keep the tapas quality intact – from the Roquefort crêpes to the spinach croquettes.

Ganbara, Calle San Jeronimo 21, San Sebastián Tel: 943 422575
A feast for the eyes and the gastronomic imagination, this is one of the old quarter's most popular pintxos bars.

Kursaal, Avenida de la Zurriola 1, Gros, San Sebastián Tel: 943 003162
Sophisticated tapas are served in this seaside cafeteria inside Rafael Moneo's truly magnificent Kursaal.

*Bar Txepetxa, Calle Pescadería 5, San Sebastián Tel: 943 422227
Manuel's family bar has been winning pintxos prizes for more than a decade – the marinated anchovies are hard to beat.

CATALONIA

Casa Alfonso, Roger de Lluria 6, Barcelona Tel: 93 301 9783
1930s Barcelona on the edge of Eixample offers quality Iberian meat tapas and luscious tortillas to famished lady-shoppers.

*Cal Pep, Plaça de les Olles 8, Barcelona Tel: 93 310 7961
A landmark bar where exquisite seafood tapas are served in sociable mayhem.

Can Paixano, Carrer Reina Cristina 7, Barcelona Tel: 93 310 0839
Hidden in a grid of waterside streets, one of Barcelona's most atmospheric bars attracts Cava-quaffing harbour-workers.

*Comerç24, Carrer Comerç 24, Barcelona Tel: 93 319 2102
The ultimate designer venue for the ultimate designer tapas signed by Carlos Abellan.

Convent dels Angels, Plaça dels Angels 5-6, Barcelona Tel: 93 329 0019
Barcelona designer chic has converted this old convent opposite the Modern Art Museum, backed up by Paco Guzman's fusion food.

*Bar Pinotxo, Mercat de la Boquería, stands 466-470, Rambla St Josep, Barcelona Tel: 93 317 1731.
It's hard to beat the Catalan earthiness of Pinotxo's tapas and raciones, with ingredients straight from neighbouring market stalls.

*Santa María, Carrer Comerç 17, Barcelona Tel: 93 315 1227
Paco Guzman packs in the punters in search of imaginative organic tapas.

Bar Tomas, Carrer Major de Sarria 49, Barcelona Tel: 93 203 1077
Makes Barcelona's tastiest Patatas bravas.

Vascelum, Plaça Santa María 4, Barcelona Tel: 93 319 0167
Devour your ración of chicken leg with prawns while sitting on the terrace in front of the church of Santa María.

RIOJA AND CASTILE

Restaurante El Candil, Ventura Ruiz Aguilera 14-16, Salamanca Tel: 923 217239
www.helcom.es/elcandil
A gastronomic monument near the Plaza Mayor tucks in a tiny tapas bar where victuals are washed down by excellent wines.

*José María, Cronista Lecea 11, Segovia Tel: 921 466017
From suckling pigs to complex tapas, this is Castile's foodie mecca.

*Momo, Calle San Pablo 13-15, Salamanca Tel: 923 280798
Castile's most stylish tapas bar has ironically taken root in this Renaissance city.

La Mortaraza, Calle José Jauregui 9, Salamanca Tel: 923 260021
An established venue for meaty regional cuisine, at the bar or in the restaurant. Sample morcilla (black pudding), oxtail, tongue or braised partridge.

*Casa Pali, Calle Laurel 11, Logroño Tel: 941 256795
One of dozens of tapas bars in Logroño's heaving epicentre, and one of the best.

Bar Sebas, Calle Albornoz 3, Logroño Tel: 941 220196
Stuffed peppers and Tortilla de patatas (potato omelette) are the specialities in this popular watering-hole.

La Tasquina, Calle Valdelaguila 3, Segovia Tel: 921 461954
Excellent wines, including cavas, head the menu here, joined by choice platters of cheeses, hams and sausage meats.

MADRID

*Albur, Calle Manuela Malasaña 15, Madrid Tel: 91 594 2733
Back-to-nature organic products from all over Spain are prepared in post-nueva cocina style in this easy-going tapas bar and restaurant.

Taberna de Antonio Sánchez, Calle Mesón de Paredes 13, Madrid Tel: 91 539 7826.

The capital's oldest, most arresting tavern has barely changed since 1830 and nor have its snail tapas.

*Bocaito, Calle Libertad 6, Madrid Tel: 91 532 1219

For a vast choice of Spain's top produce, this is where to go. Try a string of tostadas (canapés) of gambas (prawns), angulas (baby eels) or smoked crab pâté.

Chipén, Calle Cardenal Cisneros 39, Madrid Tel: 91 445 4385

A Chambéri hotspot for countless classic tapas, from octopus to frogs' legs, fried whitebait to Burgos black pudding.

Taberna de Dolores, Plaza de Jesus 4, Madrid Tel: 91 429 2243

Excellent tapas of top quality Spanish produce, from seafood to meats and hams.

Los Gatos, Calle Jesus 2, Madrid Tel: 91 429 3067

Madrid's night cats gravitate here to sample straightforward tapas in an eccentric haven of eclectic 1970s kitsch.

*José Luis, Calle Serrano 89, Madrid Tel: 91 563 0958

Long-established, and with a resident shoe-shiner, this is Madrid's foremost tapas and pintxos bar.

Casa Labra, Calle Tetuan 12, Madrid Tel: 91 531 0081

140 years of existence haven't altered the exquisite bacalao in batter or croquetas that attract people from miles away.

Lhardy, Carrera de San Jeronimo 8, Madrid Tel: 91 532 4200

19th-century elegance reigns in one of Madrid's most reputed restaurants. Caldo is still served at the front as a restorative, backed up by pastry-based snacks.

*Casa Matute, Plaza de Matute 5, Madrid Tel: 91 429 4384

Obey one of Joaquín Campos' 10 tapas commandments and you won't be disapppointed: Andalucia meets Madrid.

LEVANTE

Tabernas A Fuego Lento, Calle Caballeros 47, Plaza del Esparto, Valencia Tel: 96 392 1827

Plates of delicious Iberian produce are served in intimate dining areas in this contemporary tapas restaurant.

*Gambrinus, Plaza de la Reina 19, Valencia Tel: 96 392 3191

Beer flows to back up huge portions of tapas with an Anglo-Saxon twist.

*Bodeguilla del Gato, Calle Catalans 10 (Plaza Negrito), Valencia Tel: 96 391 8235

Hearty tapas and raciones with a Basque note in Valencia's nocturnal epicentre.

*Mesón de Labradores, Calle Labradores 19, Alicante Tel: 96 520 4846

The place to go in the backstreets of Alicante to sample hearty tapas fare.

*Bodega Montaña, Calle José Benlliure 69, El Cabanyal, Valencia Tel: 96 367 2314

This combined bar and bodega is a Levante landmark revered by all.

Nou Manolin, Calle Villegas 3, Alicante Tel: 96 520 0368

Queues form to grab a stool and indulge in delectable fresh seafood tapas and salads at this upmarket bar..

Mesón Pepe Juan, Calle Portalet 1, Calpe Tel: 96 583 2988

Squid, chicken livers, stuffed aubergine and tortilla are among the appetising tapas in this intact survivor of the Costa Blanca's tourist invasion.

Bar Pilar, Moro Zeit 13, Valencia Tel: 96 391 0497

An early 20th-century classic for consuming Valencia's renowned clochinas (mussels).

*Santa Companya, Calle Roteros 21, Valencia Tel: 96 392 2259

Michele Gallana has revived Valencia's longstanding Italian influences in this sharp tapas bar of the old quarter.

Bar Serranos, Calle Blanquerías 5, Valencia Tel: 96 391 7061

A popular, unpretentious tapas bar with a good seafood line-up.

Tasca Angel, Calle Purisima 1, Valencia Tel: 96 391 7835

There's little room here for anything other than appetising seafood and snail tapas.

ANDALUCIA

*Bodegas Campos, Calle Lineros 32, Cordoba Tel: 957 497500 www.bodegascampos.com

Luckily, this labyrinthine restaurant has a tavern at the entrance for lesser mortals to sample tapas portions of its epicurean delights.

*Casablanca, Calle Zaragoza 50, Seville Tel: 95 422 4698

Arguably the best of Seville's tapas bars, thanks to Manuel Zamora's gastronomic panache.

*Enrique Becerra, Calle Gamazo 2, Seville Tel: 95 421 3049

One of Seville's most highly-rated restaurants also attracts hordes of well-heeled tapas enthusiasts.

*La Eslava, Calle Eslava 5, Seville Tel: 95 490 6568

Innovative and quality-conscious, La Eslava is one of Seville's best-kept secrets.

*Bar Europa, Calle Siete Revueltas 35 (Plaza del Pan), Seville Tel: 95 422 1354

Sparkling c ava washes down the Catalan-influenced tapas at this elegant bar.

*La Giralda, Calle Mateos Gago 1, Seville Tel: 95 422 7435

Tiled, vaulted splendour makes a characteristic Moorish backdrop to tapas consumption.

Habanilla Café, Alameda de Hércules 63, Seville Tel: 95 490 2718.

Seville's swinging youth piles into this hopping tapas bar on a nightly basis.

Casa Morales, Calle García de Vinuesa 11, Seville Tel: 95 422 1242

Gigantic earthenware jars of olive oil create the backdrop to this traditional tapas bar, barely altered since 1850. The tapas are simple but excellent.

Casa Ricardo, Calle Hernán Cortés 2, Seville Tel: 95 438 9751

Images of the Virgin Mary are plastered over the 100-year-old walls – a divine onlooker for bacalao, jamón, meatballs and croquetas.

Casa Robles, Calle Alvarez Quintero 58, Seville Tel: 95 421 3150

A family-owned foodie institution opposite the cathedral, ensuring a fast flow of quality tapas.

Sol y Sombra, Calle Castilla 149, Triana, Seville Tel: 95 433 3935

Meaty raciones are the order of the day in this atmospheric bullfighters' bar that feels like it's straight out of a film-set.

GLOSSARY OF TERMS

In collating these recipes from our favourite tapas chefs in Spain, I selected those with ingredients that were easily available beyond the Iberian frontiers. However, even these sometimes need explaining - as do some tapas terms - so use the following glossary to identify exactly what they are.

aceite de oliva - a blend of refined and virgin olive oils with far less flavour than virgin olive oil. The basic olive oil for frying.

aceite de oliva virgen - virgin olive oil with acidity levels up to 4 per cent, quite mild in flavour.

aceite de oliva virgen extra (primera presión) - extra virgin olive oil (first cold pressing) with an acidity level below 1 per cent and a distinctive flavour. Ideal for dressings and drizzlings.

alioli - similar to mayonnaise, theoretically without the egg yolk, this Catalan sauce is made from garlic, salt, oil and optional lemon juice. It is, however, hard to make without the egg yolk.

anchoas - fresh anchovies, salted anchovy fillets or fillets in oil.

bacalao - confusingly, the Spanish word refers both to fresh cod and, far more commonly, to salt cod. The latter form is omnipresent throughout the peninsula and comes in numerous qualities, dependent on origin.

boquerones -anchovies that are pickled in a wine vinegar.

butifarra - mildly peppered Catalan pork sausage, white or black in colour, sometimes including breadcrumbs and with a finer texture than *morcilla*.

cecina - cured beef, typical of León in Old Castile, where it is salted, smoked and cured. Originally made from horsemeat, it is served very finely sliced.

chorizo - spicy cooked sausage flavoured with paprika, salt, pepper and garlic. It comes in fresh, smoked or cured versions. The best is 95 per cent pork.

embutidos - a generic term for sausage meats, whether cured, cooked or fresh.

escabeche - pickling brine or marinade, usually made of oil, vinegar, peppercorns, bay leaf, and/or spices.

guindilla - the chilli pepper, which is a New World import to Spain, plays a major role in Spanish cooking. Larger ones are generally milder than smaller ones and the hottest are the dried variety. Red chillies (ripened green chillies) have a sweeter flavour.

jamón ibérico - cured ham from Iberian black-coated pigs.

jamón ibérico de bellota - Spain's top cured ham from black-coated pigs fed on acorns in the wild.

jamón serrano - mass-produced cured ham, still delicious and often used in cooked dishes, when it is more thickly sliced.

jamón de York - cooked ham

morcilla - the Spanish version of black pudding (made from pig's blood), which may contain pine nuts and/or rice. The best is from Burgos in Old Castile.

Pedro Ximénez - a very sweet sherry often used in cooking.

pil-pil - a garlic and olive oil sauce that is sometimes made green by the addition of parsley (*salsa verde*).

pimientos del piquillo - small red peppers, oozing with sweetness and flavour, that are often used in their canned incarnation as they are only grown in Navarra.

pimentón (paprika) - the Spanish have two types: *pimentón de la vera* (from Extremadura), a smoked paprika that comes in hot, sweet and sweet-sour varieties; and straightforward *pimentón*, sun-dried paprika, also in hot and sweet versions and made in Murcia.

pintxo - canapé-style tapas, originally from the Basque region.

pisto - originally from La Mancha, this is a more condensed, Iberian version of ratatouille made from fried peppers, onion, tomato, garlic, courgette, aubergine.

raciones - slightly larger portions than tapas.

requesón - a fresh curd cheese that is similar to Italian ricotta or cottage cheese.

ventresca de atún/bonito - the belly of the tuna fish, regarded as the most tender part and therefore the most sought-after. Also to be found in canned versions at speciality grocers.

vinagre - Spaniards only use wine or sherry vinegar, usually red.

Acknowledgements

I would like to thank the chefs and bar-owners featured in this book for responding so positively to my requests, collaborating with such good humour and feeding my stomach and soul so magnificently. I am also grateful to the following for their help and advice: Francoçe Butscher at Turmadrid; José Ferri at the Valencia Region Tourist Board; the San Sebastián Convention Bureau; María José Sevilla at the Spanish Embassy, London; Pilar Faro; Mar Mateo; Christopher Branton; Tamsyn Hill; Tim O'Grady; Lorna Scott-Fox and, not least, our recipe translator, Ana Sims, who succeeded with humour in the face of sometimes daunting odds. I would also like to stress my gratitude to the photographer, Jan Baldwin, who sailed through the shoots with immense serenity and humour as well as functioning successfully long into the night, and to the designer, Vanessa Courtier, for her endless enthusiasm and creative approach to this book. Thanks also to the star of recipe-testing, Diana Henry, to our spirited gourmet editor, Rebecca Spry, and to the ever-calm Nicky Collings for seeing the project through with such grace.

INDEX TO RECIPES BY INGREDIENT